cooking with **herbs**
through the seasons

cooking with herbs
through the seasons

over 75 enticing recipes for all the year round

contributing editor: Joanna Farrow

southwater

This edition is published by Southwater

Southwater is an imprint of Anness Publishing Ltd
Hermes House, 88–89 Blackfriars Road, London SE1 8HA
tel. 020 7401 2077; fax 020 7633 9499
www.southwaterbooks.com; info@anness.com

This edition distributed in the UK by
The Manning Partnership Ltd,
6 The Old Dairy, Melcombe Road,
Bath BA2 3LR;
tel. 01225 478 444;
fax 01225 478 440;
sales@manning-partnership.co.uk

This edition distributed in the USA
and Canada by
National Book Network,
4720 Boston Way,
Lanham, MD 20706;
tel. 301 459 3366;
fax 301 459 1705;
www.nbnbooks.com

This edition distributed in Australia by
Pan Macmillan Australia,
Level 18, St Martins Tower,
31 Market Street,
Sydney, NSW 2000;
tel. 1300 135 113;
fax 1300 135 103;
customer.service@macmillan.com.au

This edition distributed in
New Zealand by
The Five Mile Press (NZ) Ltd,
PO Box 33-1071 Takapuna,
Unit 11/101–111 Diana Drive,
Glenfield, Auckland 10;
tel. (09) 444 4144;
fax (09) 444 4518;
fivemilenz@clear.net.nz

Publisher: Joanna Lorenz
Managing Editor: Helen Sudell
Project Editor: Simona Hill
Designer: Nigel Partridge
Production: Joanna King

Previously published as part of a larger volume, *Herbs*

10 9 8 7 6 5 4 3 2 1

ACKNOWLEDGEMENTS

Photographers: Karl Adamson, Edward Allwright, Steve Baxter,
Nicki Dowey, James Duncan, Gus Filgate, John Freeman,
Ian Garlick, Michelle Garrett, Peter Henley, John Heseltine,
Amanda Heywood, Janine Hosegood, Andrea Jones,
Dave Jordan, Dave King, Don Last, William Lingwood,
Patrick McLeavey, Michael Michaels, Steve Moss,
Thomas Odulate, Debbie Patterson, Craig Robertson,
Sam Stowell, Polly Wreford.

Recipes: Catherine Atkinson, Alex Barker, Angela Boggiano,
Ruby Le Bois, Carla Capalbo, Lesley Chamberlain, Kit Chan,
Jacqueline Clarke, Maxine Clark Cleary, Frances Cleary,
Carole Clements, Andi Clevely, Trish Davies, Roz Denny,
Patrizia Diemling, Stephanie Donaldson, Matthew Drennan,
Joanna Farrow, Rafi Fernandez, Christine France,
Silvano Franco, Sarah Gates, Shirley Gill, Brian Glover,
Nicola Graimes, Rosamund Grant, Juliet Harbutt,
Jessica Houdret, Deh-Ta Hsiung, Shehzad Hussain,
Christine Ingram, Judy Jackson, Peter Jordan,
Manisha Kanini, Soheila Kimberley, Lucy Knox, Masaki Ko,
Sara Lewis, Patricia Lousada, Gilly Love, Norma MacMillan,
Sue Maggs, Sally Mansfield, Maggie Mayhew, Norma Miller,
Sallie Morris, Janice Murfitt, Annie Nichols, Elizabeth Lambert
Oritz, Katherine Richmond, Anne Sheasby, Jenni Shapter,
Liz Trigg, Hilaire Walden, Laura Washburn, Stuart Walton,
Steven Wheeler, Kate Whiteman, Elizabeth Wolf-Cohen,
Jenni Wright.

Stylists: Alison Austin, Shannon Beare, Madeleine Brehaut,
Frances Cleary, Tessa Evelegh, Marilyn Forbes, Annabel Ford,
Nicola Fowler, Michelle Garrett, Carole Handslip,
Cara Hobday, Kate Jay, Maria Kelly, Lucy McKelvie,
Marion McLornan, Marion Price, Jane Stevenson, Helen Trent,
Sophie Wheeler, Judy Williams, Elizabeth Wolf-Cohen.

Home Economists: Eliza Baird, Alex Barker, Julie Beresford,
Sascha Brodie, Stephanie England, Annabel Ford,
Christine France, Carole Handslip, Kate Jay, Jill Jones,
Clare Lewis, Sara Lewis, Bridget Sargeson, Joy Skipper,
Jenni Shapter, Carole Tennant.

NOTES

For all recipes, quantities are given in both metric and
imperial measures and, where appropriate, measures are also
given in standard cups and spoons. Follow one set, but not a
mixture because they are not interchangeable.

Standard spoon and cup measures are level.
1 tsp = 5ml, 1 tbsp = 15ml, 1 cup = 250ml/8fl oz

Australian standard tablespoons are 20ml. Australian readers
should use 3 tsp in place of 1 tbsp for measuring small
quantities of gelatine, cornflour, salt etc.

Medium (US large) eggs are used unless otherwise stated

CONTENTS

INTRODUCTION

Herbs have always been part of the flora of the natural landscape. They were known to our ancestors and revered for their scents, healing properties and, as knowledge of their individual qualities grew, their role in preserving and flavouring foods. In the fourteenth century, Geoffrey Chaucer described the Cook in *The Canterbury Tales* as a very able man, especially with stews, and well informed about flavourings. Many centuries earlier, the Greek epic poet Homer depicted the heroes of the Trojan war feasting on mutton flavoured with oregano and cumin. The ancient Roman gourmet Apicius, arguably the author of the world's first cookbook, gave details of herb-flavoured sauces, as well as a recipe for a kind of ham *en croûte*, flavoured with honey and bay leaves, and many ancient Egyptian tombs depict herbs growing and being used in a multitude of ways.

It is likely, therefore, that herbs, as we know them today, were as important in the kitchens of our ancestors as they are in our own. It is also possible that the range of culinary herbs quickly

Below: A traditional formal herb garden contains all the well-known herbs.

extended well beyond native species. Crusaders and explorers are recorded as having returned home with exotic spices and medicinal herbs, just as the early settlers journeyed to America taking with them the familiar herbs and flowers from their gardens that would remind them of their homelands.

WHAT ARE HERBS?

Definitions of what constitutes a herb have changed radically over the centuries as plant knowledge and identification have improved. Throughout the Middle Ages, the term "herb" referred to any edible plant that grew above the ground, whether parsley or cabbage. (Edible plants growing underground were known collectively as "roots".) Another definition described herbs as plants that produce leaves, seeds or flowers used for flavouring food, making medicines or creating perfumes. All shrubs with woody stems or that are evergreen, such as rosemary, thyme and sage, were excluded. Clearly this definition was inadequate. Even today there is still some confusion. Garlic, for example, is used as a flavouring, although it certainly isn't green and neither does it grow above ground. Some would class this bulb

Above: Many fresh herbs can be preserved by drying to extend their use.

along with onions and leeks as a vegetable. Chives, on the other hand, another member of the same *Allium* family, are almost invariably considered to be a herb.

A herb is now understood to mean a plant, of which some part of its root, stem, leaves, flowers, or fruits are used for their scent, for medicine or for flavouring food. This broad-ranging definition includes flowers such as nasturtium: the flowers can be added to salads along with the delicious peppery-tasting leaves, and they also have antibacterial and antiseptic properties.

It also includes bulbs such as onions, fruits such as figs which have a medicinal and culinary purpose, roots such as horseradish, as well as the narrower band of green, leafy plants traditionally associated with the herb family. Whatever the anomalies in their definition, there is no doubt that herbs add immeasurably to the pleasure of eating. Their fragrance and flavour enhance other ingredients and give piquancy and character to both sweet and savoury dishes.

FRESH HERBS

Freshly picked herbs have the best flavour – not necessarily the strongest, but the most subtle, with resonant undertones. Herbs picked and put straight into the cooking pot have more nutritional value and a fuller flavour than those that are dried or freeze-dried, since the essential oils contained in the leaves won't have had time to evaporate between picking and cooking.

If you can grow your own herbs, it is well worth doing so. Most require a fairly sunny site, light, well-drained soil, that is not too rich in nutrients, and many are drought tolerant. A relatively small space in the garden can accommodate a good selection of basic kitchen herbs, such as basil, chives, coriander (cilantro), dill, marjoram or oregano, parsley, sage, tarragon and thyme. Pots on a patio or balcony are

perfect for a small bay tree, a rosemary bush and a tub of mint, which is best grown in a container as it can be invasive if allowed to grow freely.

For those without gardens, an outdoor window box or a few pots on the kitchen windowsill can still provide space to grow your favourites. Most supermarkets sell pots of common herbs and they can also be bought from garden suppliers. Herbs are at their most scented first thing in the morning before the sun has

Above: A modern herb wheel makes a strong focal point in a large garden.

brought heat to the leaves and the essential oils have evaporated, or last thing in the evening when the sun has subsided.

Fresh herbs can be stored in the refrigerator for a few days. Wrap small bunches in damp kitchen paper, place in a plastic bag and store in the salad drawer. Place larger bunches in water and keep in the refrigerator or in a cool

Below: Commercially dried poppy seeds are for use whole or ground in breads, biscuits, bakery products and as a garnish.

Below: Fresh basil leaves have an affinity with tomatoes and aubergines (eggplant), and add fragrance to ratatouille, pasta and pesto sauces.

Below: Sunflower seeds are eaten fresh or roasted in salads and breads. Oil, made from the seeds, is used for cooking and in salad dressings.

Above: Parsley is best used fresh. It doesn't retain its flavour when dried. Parsely is a popular culinary herb which complements the flavour of fish.

Above: Borage flowers have a taste of cucumber and can be added to fruit drinks and wine cups. The flowers make an attractive salad garnish.

Above: Lemon balm adds a lemon flavour to desserts, cordials, liqueurs and wine cups, salads, soups, sauces, stuffings, poultry, game and fish.

place away from direct sunlight. Packets of fresh herbs from the supermarket can be useful for specific dishes. If you are cooking only one exotic dish in the week, these are the solution to providing authentic flavours.

DRIED HERBS

As the recipes in this book are specific to the seasons, and making the most of seasonal produce, fresh herbs are recommended throughout. However, dried herbs are useful store-cupboard (pantry) items for those times when you run out of fresh herbs. They are far more pungent, although less subtle than fresh, so use only about one-third of the quantity. Freeze-dried herbs retain more of their natural flavour than air-dried ones. Those with a high oil content, such as rosemary and bay, can be dried more satisfactorily than more delicate herbs, such as basil and chervil.

Dried herbs lose their flavour quite quickly, so buy in only small quantities and regularly check infrequently-used herbs. In any case, discard any unused dried herbs after 6–9 months. Store in airtight, glass containers in a cool, dark place.

DRYING HERBS

If you have a glut of herbs at any time, you could try drying some to preserve them for use in the late autumn and winter when fresh herbs are less

plentiful and there are less varieties for harvesting. It is easy to dry your own herbs. Choose stems that look healthy and pick them early in the morning after the dew has dried. Lavender flowers should be harvested before the flowers open. Tie your herbs in loose bunches and hang them upside down in a well-ventilated, cool place. Alternatively, spread them out on a rack and dry them overnight in the oven on its

Below: Bouquet garni is a traditional addition to stews and casseroles. Traditionally it should include parsley, thyme and a bay leaf.

lowest possible setting. Herbs can also be dried in the microwave. Spread out sprigs on kitchen paper, cover with more kitchen paper and microwave on a high setting for 2 minutes. Rearrange the sprigs, cover with fresh paper and repeat the process. Continue, checking the herbs every 30 seconds and removing individual sprigs as soon as they are dry. Strip the leaves from the stems and store them in airtight jars, preferably in a dark place where the light won't make them deteriorate.

Opposite: A freshly-gathered collection of herbs ready to be dried.

PREPARING LEAFY HERBS

There are several different ways of preparing leafy herbs. The technique used depends on the individual characteristic of the herb, its culinary use and whether it is fresh or dried.

Washing and Drying

Leafy herbs must be carefully washed and dried before use. Wash them under cold running water to dislodge any dirt or insects then shake them as dry as possible. To dry them completely place the leaves flat on a paper towel, cover with another one, then press gently. Alternatively leave them to dry on a wire rack.

Stripping Herbs from their Stems

For woody-stemmed herbs, the leaves can be stripped from the stems before use. Hold the sprig at the tip and strip off the leaves with a fork. This technique can also be used to remove the leaves from dried herb sprigs. Strip large leaves from the stems using your fingers. Discard the stems.

COOK'S TIP
If you are not ready to use a freshly picked herb immediately, submerge the cut ends in cold water and store in a cool place. Alternatively, you can wrap the leaves loosely in a plastic bag and chill in the refrigerator.

Above: A mezzaluna is useful for chopping large quantities of herbs.

Snipping

To prepare chives snip (chop) them directly into a container. Hold the stems in one hand and, using kitchen scissors, snip the chives into pieces.

Tearing

Soft, fragrant leaves like basil should be removed from the stalks and torn directly into the dish when used for salads, dressings and sauces. Basil should never be chopped with a knife or cut with scissors – this will bruise the leaves, removing the essential oils and will make the flavour of the herb bitter. Tearing will maintain the beautiful colour of the leaves, whereas chopping will blacken them. Pick the leaves from the plant at the last minute and add to the dish just before serving so that none of the delicious flavour is lost.

Chopping

Herbs can be chopped coarsely or finely depending on personal preference, and according to the dish they are to be used in. Remove any coarse stalks and gather the herbs into a tight clump with one hand while you chop with the other. Then chop with both hands on the knife until they are sufficiently fine.

Slicing

Large, soft-leafed herbs like lovage, sorrel, basil and rocket (arugula) can be finely sliced, either for garnishing or so that their flavours can be readily released into dishes such as salads, soups and sauces. Wash the leaves if necessary, pat them dry and remove the stalks. Stack them on top of one another and roll up tightly. Slice finely using a chopping knife.

Crumbling Dried Leaves

Once thoroughly dried and ready for storing, herbs should crumble readily between the fingers. Work over a sheet of paper or a small bowl. If the herbs are coarse, use a food processor, or put them in a small plastic bag and crush them with a rolling pin. Store the crumbled herbs in a dark container with a sealed lid. Keep in a cool place away from moisture.

Bruising

To release the flavour of any herbs into dishes that are cooked quickly, the herbs can be bruised first. Use a mortar and pestle to lightly crush the whole leaves or sprigs just before adding them to a dish.

Making a Bouquet Garni

A bouquet garni is useful when you want the flavour of the herbs but do not want them to show in the finished dish. A classic bouquet garni comprises parsley stalks, a sprig of thyme and a bay leaf tied together with string, although you can tailor the contents to suit your personal preference or the dish you are cooking, omitting some ingredients and adding more of others. Other vegetables or herbs you may like to include are a piece of celery stick for poultry dishes; a rosemary sprig for beef or lamb; or a piece of fennel or leek, or a strip of lemon zest, to flavour fish dishes.

1 Bundle the selection together and tie firmly with string.

Garnishing

Small sprigs, cut at the last minute from the tips of the herbs make pretty garnishes. Alternatively, pick the small whole leaves from herbs such as mint, basil and parsley and scatter over the dish just before serving, handling them as little as possible.

Once it has been used to flavour a soup, stew or casserole, fish it out with a spoon.

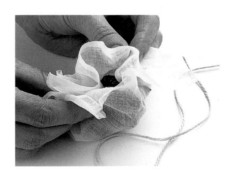

2 Another way to make a bouquet garni is to wrap the herbs in squares of muslin. This is a good choice where the herbs may be dried or crumble easily. Break or tear the herbs into small pieces and place in the centre of a 10–13cm/4–5in square of clean muslin. Bring the edges of the muslin up over the herbs and tie firmly into a bag with a length of string.

3 Use the string to tie the bundle to the pan handle, making it easy to remove. Make muslin bundles in batches so that they are readily at hand for cooking.

PREPARING VEGETABLE HERBS AND BULBS

The definition of what constitutes a herb is broad and wide-ranging. It is not just green leafy herbs such as parsley, rosemary, bay and thyme that we readily acknowledge as being herbs that fit the definition. It may be surprising to know that many vegetables such as cucumbers, peppers and artichokes, bulbs such as onions and garlic, flowers like marigolds, cowslip and lavender, seeds such as sunflower and poppy, and fruits such as fig and lemon, also fit under the broad umbrella of a herb. Paramount among these are members of the allium family – onions, shallots, garlic, spring onions (scallions) – and the capsicum family, notably (bell) peppers and chillies. Knowing how to prepare these commonly used ingredients will ensure the best results.

Seeding Chillies

Slit the chilli lengthways, open it out then scoop out and discard the seeds. Raw chillies contain volatile oils which irritate sensitive skin such as lips and the area around the eyes, so take care when handling them. Either use protective gloves or make sure you wash your hands thoroughly afterwards. Alternatively, slice the chilli into fine rings and scatter over the dish.

Roasting Peppers

Peppers are such a versatile vegetable. They can be eaten raw in salads (washed, sliced and with the seeds removed), or cooked in many different ways, such as stuffed with a delicious filling of rice and vegetables. Roasting (broiling) peppers under the grill (broiler) brings out their natural sweet flavour more than any other method of cooking.

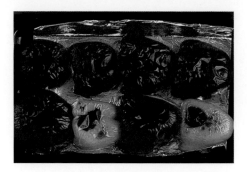

Cut the bell peppers in half and remove the seeds, membrane and stalk. Place on a baking sheet skin-side up and either cook under a hot grill, or in the oven until the skins are blackened. Remove from the heat.

USING GARLIC

Part of the allium family, garlic adds an unmistakable and delicious, pungent flavour to foods. It can also be eaten cooked or raw, although a little goes a long way. Most recipes call for just one or two cloves from the bulb to be used.

To break up the bulb, push the tip of a knife through the outer papery layer of the bulb between two cloves. Use the opening to lever the bulb apart. The cloves will come away easily.

Peeling Garlic Cloves

Each clove of garlic has a fine skin that must be removed. The easiest way to peel garlic is to place it on a chopping board and use the flat side of a wide-bladed knife to crush the clove. Place the blade flat on the clove and press it down firmly with your fist or the heel of your hand, breaking the skin of the garlic. The skin will then peel off easily. This also bruises the garlic, which allows the flavour to come out.

Chopping and Crushing Garlic

1 For a mild flavour, cut the garlic into thin slices, across the clove, or chop the clove roughly.

2 For a stronger flavour, crush the garlic rather than chop it. To make a paste you can use a mortar and pestle or a garlic press, or you can simply crush the garlic with the flat blade of a knife.

Roasting Garlic

Garlic can be roasted in much the same way as peppers, either by placing the whole bulb under a heat source or by placing the individual cloves under the heat. Roasting reduces the strength of flavour of the herb, leaving a sweetly aromatic herb. Once roasted, squeeze the garlic out of the skins for a delicious purée to add to salsas, dressings and dips.

Peeling Shallots

If you are peeling a lot of shallots, it is easier if you blanch them first in boiling water. Cut off the neck of each shallot and cut a thin slice off the bottom, but leave the root base intact. Place in a bowl and add enough boiling water to cover. Leave for about 3 minutes, drain, then slip the shallots out of their skins.

Peeling Onions

The easiest way to peel an onion is to cut off the top and bottom. Slit the skin and peel it off with your fingers.

Chopping Onions

Onions can be tricky to cut as they can slip about if you are not careful. First, slice the onion in half from top to bottom and place it cut-side down. Slice across the onion, leaving a small section uncut at the root end, then slice down through the onion at right angles to these cuts from neck to root.

Minty Fresh Breath
To stop your breath smelling after eating onions, try rubbing the soles of your feet with pure peppermint oil. Within 30 minutes the smell on your breath should be mint.

Above: To remove the smell of garlic from your hands, sprinkle them with salt, then rinse in cold water before washing them with hot water and soap.

Leave the root end uncut to prevent the onion falling apart. Slice across the onion at right angles to the second set of cuts.

Watering Eyes
Chopping onions makes you cry because this action releases the volatile chemicals that give onions their strength. An old wives' tale suggests that if you bite on a crust of bread while preparing onions, then you won't cry. Perhaps the crust forms a barrier to prevent the onion's water vapour from reaching your nose and eyes.

COOK'S TIP
It is unwise to prepare any members of the onion family too far in advance. Raw alliums can develop "off-flavours" due to sulphur compounds that are released when their cell walls are broken.

PREPARING AROMATIC INGREDIENTS

Aromatic spices, leafy herbs, seeds, flower petals, fruits and nuts all have their own distinct flavours that will add colour, texture, and vital flavour to food.

PREPARING SEEDS, SPICES AND NUTS

The seeds of many herbs are used in food preparation either whole, lightly crushed or ground into powder. They can also be gently roasted or dry-fried to enhance their flavour. Similarly, most nuts are available whole, chopped or ground, or, in the case of almonds, flaked (sliced), and they too can be roasted to emphasize their flavours.

Roasting Seeds

Seeds like coriander, mustard, fennel, cumin and caraway can be lightly roasted before crushing and using, to bring out their flavours. Heat a small, heavy pan over a moderate heat for about 1 minute. Add the seeds and dry-fry them, shaking the pan constantly for a couple of minutes until the aroma starts to rise. Watch the pan, as the seeds will soon start to burn.

Grinding Seeds and Nuts

Although most herb and spice seeds can be purchased ready ground as powder, there is nothing quite so fragrant as the aroma of freshly ground

seeds. Small, easily ground seeds such as cumin, fennel and caraway can be crushed using a pestle and mortar. Place a small amount, about a tablespoon or two, in the mortar and grind in a circular motion. Some harder seeds, such as coriander, can be ground in a spice or pepper mill. Some people prefer to use a coffee grinder; grind the seeds in short bursts.

Grating Nutmeg

Nutmeg is widely available, both whole and ground, but as the flavour of the powder deteriorates quickly, it is worth buying a whole one and storing it in an airtight container. Grate (shred) the amount needed using a fine grater.

Chopping Nuts

Nuts are widely sold whole, chopped or ground and there is probably not much need to process them yourself. But if you do have a fresh supply and want to chop or grind them, do this in a food processor. The flavour will be so much better than commercially packed ones.

Roasting Nuts

Nuts, like seeds, can be roasted to accentuate their flavour. Place them in a pan over a moderate heat until lightly browned.

Infusing Saffron

Saffron threads are always infused in warm water before use to release their wonderful aroma and yellow colour. Warm a little water, add the saffron and leave to infuse (steep) for about 5 minutes. You can use both the strands and the liquid in the recipe.

Infusing Vanilla

Vanilla pods (beans) impart a sweet aromatic flavour to foods. They are generally used whole and most commonly in milk or sugar. To flavour sugar for use in custards and desserts, simply pour sugar into a clean, dry screwtop jar. Add a whole pod, then seal the jar. Leave for a few weeks before using.

To flavour milk and cream for use in ice creams and custards, add a whole vanilla pod to a pan of milk. Heat the milk with the vanilla pod until just boiling, then remove from the heat. (To intensify the flavour split the pod lengthways.) Cover and infuse for 10 minutes. Remove and discard the pod.

Savoury sauces can be infused in the same way, using herbs that complement the main ingredient – parsley sauce is the best known, although the herb remains in the sauce.

Preparing Fresh Root Ginger

This spice is one of the oldest cultivated and most popular medicinal herbs. Its unmistakable hot, fragrant and peppery taste is used in a huge variety of sweet and savoury dishes, such as tisanes, soups, stir-fries, curries, grains, desserts and cakes. More often than not it is ground ginger that is used in recipes, but finely grated (shredded) ginger can also be used.

1 Fresh root ginger is most easily peeled using a vegetable peeler or a small, sharp paring knife.

2 Chop ginger using a sharp knife to the size specified in the recipe.

3 Grate ginger finely – a box grater works well. Freshly grated ginger can also be squeezed to release the juice.

Above: Lavender flowers are one of the most versatile herbs.

FLOWERS

Many flowers add delicate flavour and beautiful colour to summer salads, desserts and cakes. Harvest herb flowers carefully as they tend to be delicate and only pick when dry or they will collapse. Gently pull the flowers from the stems.

Infusing Floral Herbs

Lavender flowers can be added to sugar in the same way as vanilla pods, or heated with liquid to impart their essential aroma.

HERB OILS AND VINEGARS

Flavouring culinary oils and vinegars with fresh herbs is an easy yet wonderful way to enjoy their flavours right through the winter months. They also make perfect gifts, presented in attractive bottles or jars. After making up bottles of oil, store in a cool place for at least a couple of weeks before use so that the herby flavours are absorbed, after which the flowers should be removed. Drain the oil through muslin, and pour the liquid into clean bottles, after which it will be good for three to six months. Herb oils are delicious for cooking chicken and fish, flavouring soups and breads and drizzling on to pizzas and roasted vegetables, while the vinegars add a refreshing tang to sauces and salad dressings and are great for zipping up syrupy desserts.

VARIATIONS
Mixed Herb Oils Try combining several herbs in one bottle. Rosemary, bay, thyme, marjoram and oregano are delicious together. Lemon, orange or lime slices add a refreshing tang to any of the combinations.
Spiced Herb Oils For a spicy flavour, add any of the following – cinnamon sticks, dried chillies, whole cloves, mace blades, cardamom pods, coriander seeds or peppercorns.
Garlic-infused Herb Oils Used sparingly, garlic adds a delicious flavour to oil. Peel several cloves, put in a small pan and just cover with the oil you are using for bottling. Poach very gently for about 25 minutes. Leave to cool then drain the garlic. Fill clean, dry bottles with the infused oil.

WARNING

There is some evidence that oils containing fresh herbs and spices can grow harmful moulds, especially once the bottle has been opened and the contents are not fully covered by the oil. To protect against this, it is recommended that the herbs and spices are removed once their flavour has passed to the oil.

HERB OILS

Strongly flavoured herbs such as thyme, bay, basil, rosemary, marjoram, oregano, sage and tarragon are particularly suited to flavouring oils, and in some cases the flowers work well too. Use a single herb or a mixture of two or more and add additional ingredients like garlic and chilli for a more robust flavour. Choose oils, like light olive oils, sunflower oil and grapeseed oil, that will not overpower the herbs. The paler the colour of the oil, the more the herbs will show through – worth bearing in mind if giving as presents. Once made for a couple of weeks, check the intensity of the flavour. If too indistinct (remember it will be further diluted once used in cooking) remove the sprigs and add fresh ones to the jar.

Aromatic Herb Oil

Use your favourite herb to flavour this delicious oil for use in salad dressings or for cooking.

MAKES ABOUT 600ML/1 PINT/2½ CUPS

INGREDIENTS
    Several large sprigs of rosemary,
        thyme, oregano, tarragon or sage
    4 bay leaves
    about 600ml/1 pint/2½ cups light
        olive oil or sunflower oil, or a
        mixture of the two

1 Wash the herbs and pat dry, discarding any damaged parts. Push the herbs down into clean, dry bottles so the tips face upwards. Don't cram too many into a small space.

2 Fill the bottles up to the necks with the oil and cover with the cork.

Basil Oil

When making basil oil the leaves can be lightly bruised to bring out the flavour. If you like, use garlic-infused (steeped) oil instead of natural olive oil for a delicious Mediterranean flavour.

MAKES 450ML/¾ PINT/ SCANT 2 CUPS

INGREDIENTS
    handful of basil leaves, about
        15g/½ oz/½ cup
    450ml/¾ pint/scant 2 cups olive oil

1 Bruise the basil leaves lightly using a mortar and pestle, then stir in a little of the oil.

2 Transfer the mixture to a clean, dry bottle and pour over the remaining oil. Cover with a lid or cork and store in a cool place for 2–3 weeks.

3 To remove the basil leaves and replace with fresh sprigs for decoration, line a sieve with muslin and drain the oil into a jug (pitcher). Allow all the oil to soak through before removing the leaves from the sieve.

4 Discard and pour the oil back into the jar. Add fresh leaves. Cover with a lid or cork and store in a cool place.

Marjoram Flower Oil

Use this fragrant oil to cook an aromatic, vegetable-filled omelette or mix with breadcrumbs and garlic to top baked vegetables.

MAKES 450ML/¾ PINT/SCANT 2 CUPS

INGREDIENTS
    30–40 marjoram flower clusters,
    clean, dry and free of insects
    450ml/¾ pint/scant 2 cups olive oil

1 Fill a large, clean, dry jam jar with the flower clusters (do not worry about removing any small leaves).

2 Cover with the olive oil, making sure the flowers are submerged. Cover with a lid and leave in a warm place for two weeks, shaking the jar occasionally.

3 Line a small sieve with clean muslin or a coffee filter bag and position over a jug (pitcher). Use to strain the oil.

4 Pour the oil into a cleaned, attractive bottle with a 450ml/¾ pint/ scant 2 cups capacity. Cover with a lid or cork and store in a cool, dry place for 3–6 months.

Above: For very strong herbs such as chillies and garlic, use rich nut oils. For more delicate ones use light olive oil.

Below: Try any flowers that you have an abundance of. Thyme, rosemary, lavender, mint and basil are all delicious.

HERB VINEGARS

Many herbs and their flowers make delicious vinegars as their flavours are very readily absorbed. Basil, rosemary, thyme, bay, tarragon, dill, mint and even rose petals give good results. Red or white wine vinegar, sherry or cider vinegars all work equally well although a richly coloured, red wine vinegar might obscure the sprigs of herbs in the bottles. Do not use an untreated aluminium pan for heating the vinegar as it might impart a metallic taste.

Aromatic Vinegar

Garlic, lemon, bay and a good-quality vinegar provide a well-flavoured base for your choice of herb.

MAKES 600ML/1 PINT/2½ CUPS

INGREDIENTS
   15ml/1 tbsp mixed peppercorns
   2 lemon slices
   4 garlic cloves, peeled
   small handful of basil, rosemary, thyme or tarragon sprigs
   3 bay leaves
   600ml/1 pint/2½ cups good-quality vinegar

1 Put the peppercorns, lemon slices and garlic cloves into a clean, dry bottle with a capacity of about 600ml/1 pint/2½ cups. (Alternatively use two smaller bottles.)

2 Push herb sprigs into the bottles with the tips facing upwards. Add the bay leaves.

3 Fill the bottles up to the necks with the vinegar. Cover with a lid or cork and store in a cool place for 2 weeks, then remove the herbs.

Rosemary-infused Vinegar

Heating the vinegar for infusing (steeping) the herbs makes a strong-flavoured herb vinegar that is ready for almost immediate use.

MAKES 600ML/1 PINT/2½ CUPS

INGREDIENTS
   600ml/1 pint/2½ cups white wine or cider vinegar
   90ml/6 tbsp chopped fresh rosemary, plus several whole sprigs

1 Bring the vinegar just to the boil in a large pan. Pour over the chopped rosemary in a bowl. Cover and leave to infuse (steep) for 3 days.

2 Strain the vinegar through a muslin-lined sieve into a large jug (pitcher). Pour into a 600ml/1 pint/2½ cup clean, dry bottle or two smaller bottles. Push several sprigs of rosemary, tips facing uppermost, into the bottle for decoration. Fit with a stopper or cork. Use immediately if you keep the herbs in the vinegar or store for up to 6 months without the herbs.

Below: Rosemary is one of the most useful culinary herbs.

Mint Flower Vinegar

This makes a lovely vinegar for a summery salad dressing.

MAKES 450ML/¾ PINT/SCANT 2 CUPS

INGREDIENTS
   large handful of mint flowers with stems and leaves attached
   450ml/¾ pint/scant 2 cups white wine or cider vinegar
   extra mint flowers for decoration

1 Put the flowers in a large, clean jar or a wide-necked bottle. Bring the vinegar to the boil, then pour over the flowers.

2 Cover and leave for 3 to 4 weeks. Remove the flowers and pour the vinegar into a clean 450ml/¾ pint/scant 2 cup jar or bottle. (An empty vinegar bottle or pickle jar can also be used.) Fit with a lid or stopper and store in a cool place.

VARIATION
Spiced Herb Vinegar
Use a mixture of spices like cinnamon sticks, allspice berries, mace blades, cardamom pods and coriander or cumin seeds.

Thyme and Raspberry Vinegar

Fruit and herbs always make a delicious marriage of flavours. This rich, sweet and fragrant vinegar gives a summery freshness to fruity salads and can be used to deglaze the pan when making game and poultry dishes.

MAKES 750ML/1¼ PINTS/3 CUPS

INGREDIENTS
  600ml/1 pint/2½ cups red wine vinegar
  15ml/1 tbsp pickling spice
  450g/1lb/2⅔ cups fresh raspberries
  small handful of fresh thyme sprigs, preferably lemon thyme

1 Put the vinegar and pickling spice into a pan and heat gently for 5 minutes. Put the raspberries in a bowl.

2 Pour the vinegar over the raspberries. Stir in the thyme, then cover and leave in a cool place to infuse (steep) for 2 days, stirring occasionally.

3 Remove the thyme sprigs and strain the vinegar through a large plastic sieve into a large jug (pitcher). Pour into clean, dry bottles and seal with a stopper or cork.

Rose-petal Vinegar

Use this delicately rose-flavoured vinegar in a dressing for light summer salads.

MAKES 300ML/½ PINT/1¼ CUPS

INGREDIENTS
  4 large red or pink unsprayed roses
  300ml/½ pint/1¼ cups white wine or cider vinegar
  rose petals, for decoration (optional)

1 Choose an unblemished rose, then gently pull the rose petals from the flower-heads. Scald the vinegar by bringing it almost to boiling point. Allow to cool.

Below: Rose-petal vinegar.

2 Chop off any damaged parts of the petals and put the petals in a large, clean, dry glass jar or bottle. Add the cooled vinegar, cover with a stopper or cork and store in a sunny position for about three weeks before using.

3 Strain the vinegar into a clean jar and discard the petals.

HERB TEAS AND TISANES

Well before the arrival of tea from China, people had discovered that infusing (steeping) the leaves, fruit and flowers of almost any edible plant in boiling water produced a refreshing, flavoursome drink which was easy, quick, free and in most cases beneficial to their health. These herbal drinks, or "tisanes", have enjoyed a remarkable revival as both supermarkets and tea specialists cater to our desire to experiment with an ever-increasing range of healthy alternatives to coffee and traditional tea.

Almost any herbs and herb flowers can be used, and the technique is generally the same. Several sprigs of the freshly picked herb are steeped in a cup of hot, but not boiling water, and left for several minutes to infuse. Remove the leaves by straining through a sieve. Serve hot or cold with honey, lemon or sugar, if you like.

MEDICINAL TISANES

Many tisanes are used as much for their therapeutic qualities as they are for their refreshing flavour. Rosemary is said to stimulate the circulation and alleviate migraine. Lavender, hyssop, thyme and marjoram infused together in a pot are taken as a remedy for cold symptoms, and hops, chamomile and lime flower are used to help beat insomnia. Peppermint is an excellent aid to digestion.

Above: Lavender tisane has an uplifting, sweet scent.

Left: Lime-blossom tisane will ensure a good night's sleep.

Lavender Tisanes

Put three sprigs of lavender flower-heads in a heatproof glass cup or mug and pour boiling water over. Leave to infuse (steep) for about 4 minutes, stirring the sprigs frequently, then remove them and serve warm or cold, sweetened with a little honey, if you like.

To make a soothing brew to relieve a headache, mix 2.5ml/½ tsp of dried lavender with 5ml/1 tsp of wood betony. Top up with hot water and leave to infuse for 10 minutes. Strain and drink.

Rose-petal Tea

A mixture of dried rose petals and China tea makes a highly scented and refreshing drink. It looks lovely served unstrained in small glasses so the petals can be seen in the base.

MAKES 130G/4½OZ

INGREDIENTS
    15g/½oz dried, scented red or pink
      unsprayed rose petals
    115g/4oz oolong or other mild- to
      medium-strength China tea

1 Mix the rose petals with the tea and store in an airtight container.

2 Make as for ordinary tea, and serve without milk.

Below: Mix dried rose petals with oolong tea and store in an airtight container in a dark place.

Left: Rose petals add a distinctive scent to tea.

Iced Apple-mint Tea

A jug (pitcher) of iced tea can be stored overnight in the refrigerator for a refreshing, summery thirst quencher.

MAKES 900ML/1½ PINTS/3¾ CUPS

INGREDIENTS
    15ml/1 tbsp Indian tea
    60ml/4 tbsp chopped fresh mint
    15ml/1 tbsp caster (superfine) sugar
    300ml/½ pint/1¼ cups clear
      apple juice
    ice cubes and sprigs of mint to serve

1 Put the tea and chopped mint in a pot or large jug and add 750ml/1½ pints/ 3 cups boiling water. Leave to infuse (steep) for 5 minutes.

2 Strain into a jug and stir in the sugar. Leave to cool. Add the apple juice and chill until ready to serve.

3 Serve in tall glasses with ice cubes and sprigs of mint.

Below: Chamomile, with its pretty, daisy-like flowers, is one of the better-known herbs. Taken in tea, it helps to assist digestion and settle nerves and anxiety leading to peaceful sleep.

VARIATIONS

Chamomile Tisane Infuse (steep) three or four flower-heads in hot but not boiling water as for Lavender Tisane. Do not infuse them for too long as the drink might become bitter.

Hyssop Tisane Make as above, using one sprig of flowering hyssop.

Lemon Verbena Tisane Take a flowering spray of lemon verbena and a couple of leaves and infuse.

Lime-blossom Tisane Use lime flowers as they begin to open. Steep five or six flowers for each cup and add hot, but not boiling water.

Peppermint Tisane Make as above, infusing one large sprig of peppermint leaves and flowers.

Chamomile and Peppermint Tisane Mix together 75g/3oz dried chamomile flowers and 25g/1oz dried peppermint leaves. Store and use as Rose-petal Tea.

Lemon Balm and Ceylon Tea Mix together 25g/1oz dried lemon balm and 115g/4oz Ceylon tea. Store and use as for Rose-petal Tea.

Marigold and Verbena Tisane Mix together 50g/2oz dried marigold petals and 25g/1oz dried lemon verbena leaves. Store and use as for Rose-petal Tea.

HERB CORDIALS AND DRINKS

From fragrant and Sparkling Elderflower Drink to smooth, tangy Rosehip Cordial, herbs and flowers can be used as a base for an interesting assortment of drinks, and as a lively addition to various fruit, vegetable and dairy-based drinks. Fruit and herbs can be infused (steeped) in alcohol to create an irresistibly punchy tipple, or steeped in syrups to make fresh-tasting, vibrant cordials that keep for months. Many herbs, particularly those in flower, make stunning additions to fruit punches, for summer parties and barbecues.

CORDIALS

Home-made cordials have a fresh, intense flavour that can rarely be bought in a shop. They can be lavished on to scoops of fruit or vanilla ice cream, swirled into fruit compotes or salads or simply served topped up with ice-cold water or lemonade as a thirst-quenching drink.

Rosehip Cordial

Collect rosehips from the hedgerows for this delightful cordial. It makes a wonderful autumn and winter drink.

MAKES 1.75 LITRES/3 PINTS/7½ CUPS

INGREDIENTS
  1kg/2¼lb rosehips
  granulated sugar

1 Put 1.75 litres/3 pints/7½ cups water in a large, heavy pan and bring to the boil. Meanwhile blend the rosehips in a food processor until finely chopped. Add to the boiling water and return to the boil. Cover with a lid and simmer very gently for 10 minutes. Turn off the heat and leave for 15 minutes.

2 Sterilize a jelly bag by immersing it in boiling water for 2 minutes. Drain and suspend the jelly bag over a large bowl. Strain the rosehips through the jelly bag and leave overnight until the juices stop dripping through.

COOK'S TIP
Cordials can be stored, chilled in the refrigerator, for 3 weeks. Sterilize bottles before use.

3 Measure the juice and return to the pan. Add 350g/12oz/1¾ cups sugar for every 600ml/1 pint/2½ cups syrup. Heat gently, stirring until the sugar has dissolved. Bring to the boil and boil for 5 minutes, or until syrupy. Pour into thoroughly cleaned bottles and cover with stoppers or corks. Store in the refrigerator.

Below: Rosehip cordial is a healthy drink, high in vitamin C.

Rosemary, Redcurrant and Orange Cordial

Redcurrants and oranges combine with a subtle hint of rosemary to make a tangy, summery cordial.

MAKES ABOUT 900ML/1½ PINTS/3¾ CUPS

INGREDIENTS
 900g/2lb/8 cups fresh redcurrants
 8 large sprigs of rosemary
 finely grated rind and juice of
  2 oranges
 granulated sugar

1 Strip the redcurrants from their stems, put in a pan and mash lightly using a potato masher. Add the rosemary, orange rind and 300ml/ ½ pint/1¼ cups water. Bring just to the boil, then remove from the heat and leave to cool. Stir in the orange juice.

2 Sterilize a jelly bag by immersing it in boiling water for 2 minutes. Suspend the jelly bag over a large bowl. Strain the fruit and juices through the bag overnight until the mixture is dry.

3 Put the juice in a pan adding 350g/ 12oz/1¾ cups sugar for every 600ml/ 1 pint/2½ cups syrup. Heat gently until the sugar has dissolved then bring to the boil and boil for 5 minutes, or until syrupy. Pour into thoroughly cleaned bottles and cover with stoppers or corks. Store in the refrigerator.

Lemon Barley and Bay Syrup

Despite its image as a remedy for minor ailments, chilled lemon barley juice is both delicious and invigorating. The gentle earthiness of the bay leaves blend perfectly with the tangy flavour of the lemons.

MAKES 750ML/1¼ PINTS/3 CUPS

INGREDIENTS
 75g/3oz/½ cup pearl barley
 3 lemons
 4 bay leaves
 75g/3oz/6 tbsp granulated sugar
 ice cubes, lemon slices and sprigs of
  lemon balm, to decorate

Above: Fragrant herbal cordials are cool and refreshing in summer. Serve with decorative, floral ice cubes.

1 Put the pearl barley in a bowl and cover with boiling water. Stir well then rinse thoroughly until the water runs clear. Put in a pan with 1 litre/1¾ pints/ 4 cups boiling water. Bring to the boil, cover with a lid and simmer gently for 45 minutes.

2 Scrub the lemons and pare off the rind with a sharp knife. Squeeze the juice and reserve. Put the pared rind in a bowl with the bay leaves and sugar.

3 Strain the hot barley water over the sugar mixture and stir until the sugar has dissolved. Cover and leave overnight.

4 Add the lemon juice and transfer to a jug (pitcher). Chill for up to two weeks. Serve undiluted with ice, lemon slices and sprigs of lemon balm to decorate.

Basil, Tabasco and Tomato Juice

Drinks that combine herbs, fruit and vegetables are renowned for boosting health and vitality. Serve any time.

MAKES ONE GLASS

INGREDIENTS
 small handful fresh basil leaves
 5cm/2in length cucumber, roughly
  chopped
 3 vine-ripened tomatoes, roughly
  chopped
 ½ red (bell) pepper, deseeded and
  roughly chopped
 60ml/4 tbsp freshly squeezed
  orange juice
 few drops Tabasco sauce, to taste

1 Put all the ingredients, except the Tabasco in a food processor or blender and process until smooth, scraping the mixture from around the sides of the bowl.

2 Pour into a tall glass and add Tabasco to taste. Serve with ice cubes if you like.

Mint Cup

Sweet, tangy and irresistibly minty, this summer cup is perfect for *al fresco* eating and drinking.

SERVES FOUR TO SIX

INGREDIENTS
large handful fresh mint leaves
30ml/2 tbsp caster (superfine) sugar
plenty of crushed ice
30ml/2 tbsp freshly squeezed
 lemon juice
175ml/6fl oz/¾ cup freshly squeezed
 grapefruit juice
600ml/1 pint/2½ cups tonic
 water, chilled
mint sprigs and lemon slices,
 to decorate

1 Crush the mint leaves with the sugar using a mortar and pestle, or a small bowl and the back of a spoon.

2 Transfer the mixture to a serving jug (pitcher) and fill with crushed ice.

3 Add the lemon juice, grapefruit juice and tonic water.

4 Stir gently and serve decorated with sprigs of mint and lemon slices.

VARIATION
Lemon Balm, Chilli and Lime Crush
For an evening dinner party, substitute lemon balm instead of the mint leaves and use lime juice instead of the lemon. Add a few drops of chilli oil with the grapefruit juice. A splash of Tequila can be added for extra kick!

Summer Punch

Borage, cucumber and mint give a subtle but essential fragrance to a classic Pimm's drink. Let all the ingredients chill together in the jug before topping up with the alcohol at the last minute, if you have time.

SERVES FOUR TO SIX

INGREDIENTS
several sprigs of borage flowers
¼ cucumber
1 orange, scrubbed
ice cubes
¼ bottle Pimm's, chilled
several sprigs of mint or lemon balm
chilled lemonade for topping up
extra borage flowers, to decorate

1 Remove each of the borage flower-heads from the green calyx by gently easing it out. Halve the cucumber lengthways and cut into thin slices. Chop the orange into small chunks leaving the skin on.

Above: It would not be summer without a jug (pitcher) of refreshing punch, topped with fruit and chilled with ice.

2 Put the cucumber and orange in a large jug and add the ice cubes, Pimm's, mint or lemon balm and borage. Top up with lemonade and serve decorated with extra borage flowers.

Mint Flower Yogurt Drink

The familiar combination of yogurt and mint are blended here with beautifully scented raspberries. Enjoy this cooling drink on a hot summer's day.

SERVES TWO

INGREDIENTS
  250ml/8fl oz/1 cup natural (plain) yogurt
  75g/3oz/½ cup fresh raspberries
  50g/2oz/¼ cup caster (superfine) sugar
  2 sprigs flowering mint, plus extra, to decorate

Put all the ingredients in a food processor or blender with 120ml/4fl oz/½ cup chilled water. Blend until smooth. Pour into glasses and serve decorated with sprigs of flowering mint.

Above: Sparkling elderflower drink is light and refreshing, just perfect for summer, and will make an unusual addition to a special occasion.

Sparkling Elderflower Drink

Made simply from elderflowers, sugar, lemons and white wine vinegar, this sparkling drink is surprisingly potent, perfect for country weddings and other summer celebrations.

MAKES 4.5 LITRES/8 PINTS/20 CUPS

INGREDIENTS
  12 elderflower heads
  juice and finely grated (shredded) rind of 1 lemon
  30ml/2 tbsp white wine vinegar
  700g/1½lb/3½ cups caster (superfine) sugar

1 Strip the elderflower heads from the stalks and put in a very large bowl with the lemon rind, juice, vinegar, sugar and 4.5 litres/8 pints/20 cups water. Cover with muslin and leave for 24 hours.

2 Strain the mixture through a fresh piece of muslin into sterilized bottles, using a funnel. Cork the bottles and leave in a cool place for 2 weeks before drinking undiluted.

Strawberry and Lavender Gin

Flavouring gin with fruits is an ancient tradition. Lavender makes a delicate, fragrant addition.

MAKES ABOUT 750ML/1¼ PINTS/3 CUPS

INGREDIENTS
  400g/14oz/3½ cups ripe but still firm strawberries, thickly sliced
  175g/6oz/scant 1 cup caster (superfine) sugar
  8 large lavender flowers
  750ml/1¼ pints/3 cups gin

1 Place all the ingredients in a large, wide-necked jar. Cover with the lid. Leave in a cool place for one week, shaking the jar gently each day.

2 Strain the gin and return to the bottle. Chill for up to 4 months. Serve over ice or with chilled tonic water.

Above: Enjoy mint flower yogurt drink on a hot summer day, or for a refreshingly fruity breakfast drink, substitute a fresh ripe peach instead of the raspberries.

HERB PICKLES AND PRESERVES

Above: Fruits and vegetables made into savoury preserves taste better if they are left to mature.

From bottled fruits and vegetables to sweet jellies and jams, most preserves benefit from the feast of flavours provided by the herb garden. Presentation plays an important role in the making of pickles and preserves as they are frequently given as gifts. An assortment of different bottles and jars is worth collecting and saves you rooting around at the last minute looking for suitable containers.

COOK'S TIPS
• All jars and bottles should be thoroughly sterilized before using for preserves. Wash in soapy water and remove any old labels. Dry them and put in the oven set at 150°C/300°C/ Gas 2 for 15 minutes before filling.
• Cellophane jam-pot covers are ideal for all preserves except pickles as the vinegar will gradually evaporate through them and spoil the top of the pickle.
• Many preserving bottles and jars have attached lids with rubber seals. Remove the seals before sterilizing.

Spiced Pears with Ginger

Use any firm pears for this tangy, spiced preserve. It is particularly good with cold meats such as ham, gammon or smoked chicken or turkey.

MAKES 1KG/2¼LB

INGREDIENTS
    600ml/1 pint/2½ cups red wine vinegar
    rind of 1 lemon
    4cm/1½in length fresh root ginger, peeled and sliced
    1 cinnamon stick
    10ml/2 tsp whole allspice berries
    2 bay leaves
    450g/1lb/2¼ cups granulated sugar
    1kg/2¼lb pears
    cloves

1 Put all the ingredients except the pears and cloves in a large pan and heat gently until the sugar dissolves, stirring frequently.

2 Peel the pears, leaving them whole, and stud a clove into each one. Add to the vinegar and simmer very gently, covered with a lid, until the pears are very tender, about 25–30 minutes. Lift out the pears and transfer them to hot jars. Boil the syrup until slightly thickened and pour over the pears. Seal the jars immediately.

Bottled Cherry Tomatoes with Basil

Other small, well-flavoured tomatoes can be used instead of cherry tomatoes but these look particularly pretty.

MAKES 1KG/2¼LB

INGREDIENTS
    1kg/2¼lb cherry tomatoes
    5ml/1 tsp salt per 1 litre/1¾ pint/ 4 cup jar
    5ml/1 tsp sugar per 1 litre/1¾ pint/ 4 cup jar
    handful of fresh basil
    4 garlic cloves per jar

1 Preheat the oven to 120°C/250°F/ Gas ½. Prick each tomato with a wooden cocktail stick, then pack them tightly into sterilized jars with heatproof lids, adding salt and sugar as you go.

2 Fill the jars to within 2cm/¾in of the tops, tucking the basil and garlic in among the tomatoes. Rest the lids on the jars but do not seal. Stand the jars on a baking sheet lined with newspaper.

3 Place the filled jars in the oven and cook for about 45 minutes, or until the juices start simmering. Remove from the oven and seal immediately. Store and use within 6 months.

Dill Pickle

Use a glut supply of dill to make this classic preserve, delicious with both cheese and cold meats.

MAKES 3 LITRES/5¼ PINTS/12 CUPS

INGREDIENTS
675g/1½lb ridge cucumbers
large bunch fresh dill
5 garlic cloves, peeled and sliced
900ml/1½ pints/3¾ cups white
  wine vinegar
45ml/3 tbsp coarse salt
10ml/2 tsp mixed peppercorns
3 bay leaves
2 star anise

1 Trim the ends off the cucumbers and cut into 5cm/2in pieces. Place in a bowl of cold water and chill for 24 hours.

2 Drain and pierce the cucumber pieces in several places with a wooden cocktail stick.

COOK'S TIP
Add 45ml/3 tbsp sugar to the vinegar for a sweeter flavour.

3 Pack into sterilized jars with plenty of dill and the garlic. Put the vinegar in a pan with 375ml/13fl oz/scant 1⅔ cups water. Add the salt, peppercorns, bay leaves and star anise. Bring to the boil and boil for 5 minutes. Pour over the cucumbers and seal immediately.

Kashmir Chutney

Ginger, cayenne, coriander and garlic are used to flavour this traditional family recipe for chutney. Enjoy it with a cheese ploughman's or hot or cold grilled (broiled) sausages and meats.

MAKES ABOUT 2.75KG/6LB

INGREDIENTS
1kg/2¼lb green apples
15g/½ oz garlic cloves
1 litre/1¾ pints/4 cups malt vinegar
450g/1lb/3¼ cups fresh or semi-
  dried dates
115g/4oz stem ginger
450g/1lb/3¼ cups seedless raisins
450g/1lb/2 cups light muscovado
  (molasses) sugar
2.5ml/½ tsp cayenne pepper
20g/¾ oz salt
large handful fresh coriander (cilantro)

1 Core and coarsely chop the apples.

2 Peel and chop the garlic. Put the apples and garlic in a large, heavy pan with enough vinegar to cover them.

3 Boil until the apples are softened. Add the remaining ingredients, except the coriander, to the pan. Cook for 45 minutes, stirring frequently, until thickened and pulpy. Chop the coriander, stir in and cook for 2 minutes. Spoon into sterilized jars and seal immediately.

Left: Pickles add flavour to plain food.

VARIATION
Dry-fry 30ml/2 tbsp mustard seeds in a small pan until they start to pop. Use instead of the star anise.

Tomato Ketchup

Use really ripe tomatoes to give maximum flavour to this spicy sauce.

MAKES 2.75KG/6LB

INGREDIENTS
    2.25kg/5lb ripe tomatoes
    1 onion, peeled
    8 cloves
    6 allspice berries
    6 black peppercorns
    several sprigs fresh rosemary
    3 bay leaves
    25g/1oz fresh root ginger, peeled
      and sliced
    1 celery heart
    30ml/2 tbsp dark brown sugar
    65ml/4½ tbsp raspberry or red
      wine vinegar
    3 garlic cloves, peeled
    15ml/1 tbsp salt

1 Peel and halve the tomatoes and scoop out the seeds. Place the flesh in a large, heavy pan. Stud the onion with cloves and tie in a double-thickness layer of muslin with the allspice, peppercorns, rosemary, bay and ginger.

2 Chop the celery and add to the pan with the bag of spices, sugar, vinegar, garlic and salt. Bring to the boil, reduce the heat and simmer, uncovered, stirring frequently for about 1½ hours.

3 Remove the muslin bag, squeezing out the juices, and blend the tomato mixture in a food processor or blender until smooth.

4 Return to the pan and simmer for 5 minutes. Transfer to jars and store in the refrigerator for up to 2 weeks.

Mint Sauce

Home-made mint sauce is far superior to shop-bought and keeps for several months in the refrigerator. To make a 250ml/8fl oz/1 cup quantity, finely chop 1 large bunch fresh mint and put in a large bowl. Add 105ml/7 tbsp boiling water and leave to infuse (steep). When cooled to lukewarm, add 150ml/¼ pint/⅔ cup white wine vinegar and 30–45ml/2–3 tbsp caster (superfine) sugar to taste. Pour into a clean bottle or jar and store in the refrigerator.

Papaya and Lemon Relish

Although this relish makes a small quantity, its flavour is strong and a little goes a long way.

MAKES ABOUT 450G/1LB

INGREDIENTS
    1 large unripe papaya
    1 onion, thinly sliced
    40g/1½ oz/⅓ cup raisins
    250ml/8fl oz/1 cup red wine vinegar
    juice of 2 lemons
    150ml/¼ pint/⅔ cup elderflower
      cordial
    165g/5½ oz/generous ¾ cup golden
      granulated sugar
    1 cinnamon stick
    2 bay leaves
    5ml/1 tsp paprika
    2.5ml/½ tsp salt

Left: Tomato Ketchup and Mint Sauce.

1 Peel the papaya, halve lengthways and scoop out the seeds. Roughly chop the flesh and put in a heavy pan.

2 Add the onion, raisins and vinegar. Bring to the boil and simmer gently for 10 minutes. Add the remaining ingredients and bring to the boil, stirring. Reduce the heat and simmer gently for 50–60 minutes.

3 Transfer to sterilized jars, cover and store for at least 1 week before using. Chill once opened.

VARIATION
Mango and Lemon Relish Use one large, firm mango instead of the papaya.

Lavender Jelly

This pretty jelly really captures the essence of summer. Serve it with roast lamb, chicken or duck, or even with warmed scones (US biscuits) or croissants. Do not worry about peeling and coring the apples as the mixture is strained through a jelly bag.

MAKES ABOUT 1.8KG/4LB

INGREDIENTS
   1.8kg/4lb cooking apples, washed
      and roughly chopped
   105ml/7 tbsp lavender flowers,
      chopped
   about 1.3kg/3lb/6¾ cups sugar

1 Put the apples in a pan with 75ml/ 5 tbsp of the lavender flowers and 1.75 litres/3 pints/7½ cups water. Simmer gently for about 25 minutes, or until the apples are soft and mushy.

2 Sterilize a jelly bag by immersing it in boiling water for 2 minutes. Drain and suspend the jelly bag securely over a large bowl.

3 Strain the apple mixture through the bag and leave overnight until the juices stop dripping through.

4 Measure the juice and return to the pan, adding 450g/1lb/2¼ cups sugar for every 600ml/1 pint/2½ cups juice. Heat gently, stirring until the sugar has dissolved. Bring to the boil and boil until setting point is reached (see Cook's Tip).

5 Leave to cool for 15 minutes then stir in the remaining lavender flowers. Transfer to dry, sterilized jars and cover with a lid. Store in a cool place for up to 6 months.

VARIATION
Apple, Strawberry and Rosemary Jelly
Use chopped rosemary instead of the lavender and substitute 900g/ 2lb/8 cups whole strawberries for half the apples, adding them for the final 5 minutes' cooking time.

Pickled Plums de Provence

These savoury plums are transformed into an unusual accompaniment for cold roast meats by adding aromatic herbs, including rosemary, garlic and sweet lavender.

MAKES ABOUT 1.3KG/3LB

INGREDIENTS
   1.3kg/3lb firm plums
   4 sprigs rosemary
   4 bay leaves
   4 lavender flowers
   2 thyme sprigs
   4 unpeeled garlic cloves
   900ml/1½ pints/3¾ cups white
      wine vinegar
   500g/1¼ lb/2¾ cups granulated sugar

1 Prick over the plums with a wooden cocktail stick and pack them into 1 medium and 1 small Kilner jar, tucking in the herb sprigs and garlic.

2 Put the vinegar and sugar in a pan and heat gently until the sugar dissolves. Bring to the boil and boil for 5 minutes, or until syrupy. Allow to cool, then remove the herb sprigs.

3 Pour over the plums, making sure they are completely covered. Seal tightly and store in a cool place for at least 1 month before using.

COOK'S TIP
To check if jelly or jam is at setting point, put a small amount on a saucer – if it holds its shape it is ready.

Left: Lavender jelly is an unusual addition to the store cupboard (pantry).

HERB SAUCES

A well-flavoured sauce, mayonnaise or dip makes an imaginative accompaniment to serve with a variety of dishes. Tasty combinations of herbs, such as dill and capers, rosemary and onion; parsley and bay, or garlic and mixed herbs, are ideal additions to sauces to serve with plain foods.

White Sauce

This classic white sauce is an essential part of many savoury dishes. A good sauce, which is smooth, glossy and buttery, makes the perfect base to which herbs, spices and other flavours can be added (see variations).

MAKES ABOUT 600ML/1 PINT/2½ CUPS

INGREDIENTS
40g/1½ oz/3 tbsp butter
40g/1½ oz/⅓ cup plain (all-purpose) flour
600ml/1pint/2½ cups milk
good pinch of freshly grated nutmeg
30–45ml/2–3 tbsp double (heavy) cream (optional)
salt and ground black pepper

1 Melt the butter in a heavy pan over a moderate heat. Remove from the heat and stir in the flour.

2 Gradually whisk in about a quarter of the milk until completely smooth, then whisk in the remainder. Set the pan over a moderate heat and bring to the boil, whisking continuously.

3 When the sauce starts to thicken, reduce the heat to its lowest setting and cook gently, stirring frequently until smooth and glossy. Stir in the nutmeg, cream, if using, and seasoning to taste.

VARIATIONS

Cheese Sauce Add 50g/2oz/½ cup finely grated (shredded) Cheddar cheese, 5ml/1 tsp finely chopped fresh thyme and 2.5ml/½ tsp Dijon mustard at step 3 of the White Sauce recipe.

Dill and Caper Sauce Finely chop 30ml/2 tbsp capers and add to the sauce at step 3 with 30ml/2 tbsp finely chopped dill.

Egg and Chive Sauce Shell and finely chop 2 hard-boiled (hard-cooked) eggs. Add to the sauce at step 3 with 45ml/3 tbsp chopped chives.

Parsley Sauce Heat the milk in a pan with 1 bay leaf, 1 whole peeled onion and 12 black peppercorns and bring almost to the boil. Remove from the heat and leave to infuse (steep) for 20 minutes. Strain and make the white sauce as before. Stir in 60ml/4 tbsp finely chopped parsley at step 3.

Rosemary and Onion Sauce Finely chop 1 onion and sauté gently in the butter before adding the flour. Add 15ml/1 tbsp finely chopped rosemary at step 3.

COOK'S TIPS

• A white sauce can be made ahead and reheated. Transfer to a bowl, add a dot of butter and let it melt over the surface to prevent a skin forming. Leave to cool. Refrigerate for up to 2 days and reheat before serving. Alternatively place a circle of greaseproof (waxed) paper over the surface.

• The recipe for White Sauce gives a consistency suitable for pastry and pie fillings or as a topping for lasagne and crêpes.

• As an accompanying sauce to meat, fish and vegetables use 15g/½ oz/2 tbsp butter and flour.

• For a thicker sauce to use as a soufflé base or to bind ingredients together, use 50g/2oz/¼ cup butter and 50g/2oz/½ cup flour.

Bread Sauce

Bread sauce flavoured with cloves and bay leaves makes a comforting, wintry accompaniment to roast game, turkey, chicken and lamb.

SERVES SIX TO EIGHT

INGREDIENTS
1 onion, peeled
8 whole cloves
2 bay leaves
600ml/1 pint/2½ cups milk
115g/4oz/2 cups fresh breadcrumbs
15g/½ oz/1 tbsp butter
45ml/3 tbsp single (light) cream
salt and ground black pepper

1 Stud the onion with cloves and put in a pan with the bay leaves and milk. Bring to the boil, then remove from the heat and leave to infuse (steep) for 15 minutes.

2 Remove the onion and bay leaves and stir in the breadcrumbs. Simmer gently for about 10 minutes, or until thickened. Stir in the butter, cream and seasoning.

Below: Richly-flavoured bread sauce.

Herby Onion Gravy

The sage, thyme and parsley make this gravy delicious with roasts, sausages, liver and bacon, and toad in the hole. Make sure you really caramelize the onions in the oil before adding the remaining ingredients to achieve a rich flavour and deep, golden gravy.

MAKES ABOUT 900ML/1½ PINTS/3¾ CUPS

INGREDIENTS
   30ml/2 tbsp vegetable oil
   3 onions, finely sliced
   2.5ml/½ tsp caster (superfine) sugar
   10ml/2 tsp plain (all-purpose) flour
   2 sprigs each of sage, thyme
      and parsley
   900ml/1½ pints/3¾ cups chicken or
      vegetable stock
   salt and ground black pepper

1 Heat the oil in a frying pan. Add the onions and sugar and sauté gently for about 10 minutes, or until the onions are just beginning to turn golden. Sprinkle on the flour and cook, stirring for 1 minute.

2 Add the herbs and stock and bring to the boil. Reduce the heat and simmer gently, uncovered, for 5 minutes, or until slightly thickened. Season to taste.

Above: Herby onion gravy is irresistible.

Rich Tomato Sauce

Generously flavoured with Mediterranean herbs, this intensely flavoured sauce keeps well in the refrigerator for several days and makes a lovely sauce for pasta, grilled (broiled) meats and barbecues, or as a pizza topping.

SERVES FOUR TO SIX

INGREDIENTS
   45ml/3 tbsp olive oil
   2 celery sticks, finely chopped
   1 onion, finely chopped
   3 garlic cloves, crushed
   small handful of chopped mixed
      herbs, such as parsley, thyme,
      marjoram, oregano, basil
   1 bay leaf
   675g/1½lb ripe tomatoes, peeled
      and chopped
   30ml/2 tbsp sun-dried tomato paste
   150ml/¼ pint/⅔ cup vegetable stock
   salt and ground black pepper

1 Heat the oil in a pan. Add the celery and onion and fry gently for 5 minutes. Add the garlic and herbs, and fry for 2 minutes.

2 Add the tomatoes, tomato paste and stock, and bring to the boil. Reduce the heat and simmer gently for about 20 minutes, or until thickened and pulpy. Season to taste and serve hot.

Sauce Vierge

This quick sauce adds interest to fried or grilled meat and fish. Heat 60ml/ 4 tbsp extra virgin olive oil in a small pan. Add 1.5ml/¼ tsp crushed coriander seeds and fry for 1 minute. Add 5 ripe, skinned and seeded tomatoes, a small handful of chopped parsley, tarragon and chervil and a little seasoning. Cook for 30 seconds before serving.

HERBS IN SALSAS, MAYONNAISE AND DIPS

Due largely to healthy and delicious Mediterranean ingredients, such as herbs, richly flavoured olive oils and other flavourings, we have a fabulous selection of chilled, olive-oil-based sauces to choose from. Those fresh, summery tastes, from the classic mayonnaise and all its variations to thick, aromatic olive oil dressings, will quickly enliven even the simplest meat, fish and vegetable dishes. Serve them freshly made if convenient, or store in the refrigerator, covered tightly for up to 2 days.

Salsa Verde

Nothing quite epitomizes the wonderfully aromatic, intense flavour of herbs better than a freshly blended Salsa Verde. Excellent with roast or grilled (broiled) meats as well as pan-fried fish and vegetable dishes.

SERVES FOUR

INGREDIENTS
    2 garlic cloves, chopped
    25g/1oz/1 cup flat leaf parsley
    15g/½ oz/½ cup fresh basil, mint or
        coriander (cilantro), or a mixture
        of herbs
    15ml/1 tbsp chopped chives
    15ml/1 tbsp capers, rinsed
    120ml/4fl oz/½ cup extra virgin
        olive oil
    5 anchovy fillets, rinsed
    10ml/2 tsp French mustard
    a little finely grated (shredded)
        lemon rind and juice
    salt and ground black pepper

Above: Salsa verde, one of the best known and flavoursome salsas.

1 Put the first five ingredients and 15ml/1 tbsp of the oil in a blender or food processor and process lightly.

2 Gradually add the remaining oil in a thin stream with the motor running to make a thick sauce.

VARIATIONS
• For a creamier, slightly milder flavour whisk in 45ml/3 tbsp crème fraîche.
• Substitute herbs such as chervil, tarragon, dill or fennel for a sauce that goes particularly well with fish, shellfish or chicken.

3 Transfer the herb mixture to a bowl and add the lemon rind and juice, and seasoning to taste. (You might not need additional salt as the anchovies and capers are very salty.) Serve immediately or chill until required.

Fresh Mayonnaise

Mayonnaise is definitely worth making, provided you have a little time and patience. Store in the refrigerator, covered tightly for up to 1 week. Use the freshest possible eggs. Infants, the elderly and those with compromised immune systems should avoid eating foods containing uncooked eggs.

MAKES ABOUT 350ML/12FL OZ/1½ CUPS

INGREDIENTS
  2 egg yolks
  350ml/12fl oz/1½ cups olive oil
  15–30ml/1–2 tbsp lemon juice or
    white wine vinegar
  5–10ml/1–2 tsp Dijon mustard
  salt and ground black pepper

COOK'S TIP
• Mayonnaise can be made successfully in a food processor. Make exactly as above, pouring in the oil while the motor is running. If it separates beat another egg yolk. Gradually whisk in the curdled mixture as before.

1 Put the egg yolks in a bowl with a pinch of salt, and beat well.

2 Add the oil, a little at a time, beating constantly with an electric mixer or balloon whisk.

3 When a quarter of the oil has been added, beat in 5–10ml/1–2 tsp of the lemon juice or vinegar.

4 Continue beating in the oil in a thin, steady stream. As the mayonnaise thickens, add a little more lemon juice or vinegar.

5 When all the oil has been added, stir in the mustard, seasoning and a little more lemon juice or vinegar, if necessary. (If the mayonnaise is too thick, stir in a spoonful of water.) Store covered with plastic film or in an airtight container in the refrigerator.

VARIATIONS
Basil and Garlic Mayonnaise Tear a small handful each of green and opal basil leaves into small pieces and stir into the mayonnaise with 2 crushed garlic cloves.
Cucumber and Dill Mayonnaise Halve and scoop out the seeds from a 7.5cm/3in length of cucumber. Finely chop the flesh and add to the mayonnaise with 30ml/2 tbsp chopped dill.
Green Mayonnaise Add 25g/1oz/ ½ cup each of finely chopped parsley and watercress, 1 crushed garlic clove and 3 finely chopped spring onions (scallions).
Tartare Sauce Add 30ml/2 tbsp each of chopped tarragon and parsley, 15ml/1 tbsp each of chopped capers and gherkins and a dash of lemon juice or vinegar.

Left: Complete a fresh prawn salad with a creamy home-made mayonnaise.

DIPS

The simplest dips can be made by folding chopped fresh herbs into a mayonnaise, fromage frais, crème fraîche, or thick yogurt. You can also zip them up with garlic, lemon, ginger, spices and other aromatic ingredients. Serve with colourful crudités, interesting breads, or crisps.

Mellow Garlic Dip

Baking garlic until it is soft and succulent mellows its fiery, raw flavour, leaving it sweet and delicious.

SERVES FOUR

2 whole garlic heads
15ml/1 tbsp olive oil
60ml/4 tbsp mayonnaise
75ml/5 tbsp natural (plain) yogurt
5ml/1 tsp grainy mustard
salt and ground black pepper

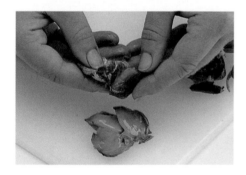

1 Brush the garlic heads with olive oil and wrap them tightly in kitchen foil. Bake at 200°C/400°F/Gas 6 for about 40 minutes, until soft to the touch. When cool enough to handle, separate the garlic cloves and remove their skins. Sprinkle the cloves with salt and mash on the chopping board with a knife, until puréed.

COOK'S TIPS

• The foil-wrapped garlic heads can also be cooked around the edges of a barbecue. Allow about 25 minutes, turning occasionally.

• Leftover dip will keep, well covered, in the refrigerator for 3–4 days. Use as a topping for baked potatoes, in sandwiches or serve with pan-fried meat or fish.

2 Put the garlic in a bowl and stir in the mayonnaise, yogurt and mustard. Beat well.

3 Check the seasoning, adding more salt and pepper to taste. Transfer to a serving bowl, cover and chill until ready to serve.

VARIATIONS

Garlic, Lovage and Apple Dip Make as above using 1 garlic head. Add 15ml/1 tbsp chopped lovage and 1 peeled and grated dessert apple.

Tarragon, Walnut and Roquefort Dip Make as above increasing the yogurt to 150g/5oz. Add 30ml/2 tbsp chopped tarragon, 25g/1oz/¼ cup finely chopped walnuts and 40g/1½oz crumbled Roquefort cheese.

Sage Flower and Garlic Dip Pull the sage flowers from the stems until you have a small handful. Add to the garlic dip with 30ml/2 tbsp chopped flat leaf parsley.

Anchovy, Olive and Basil Dip Make as above using 1 garlic head. Add 4 drained and chopped canned anchovy fillets, 10 pitted and sliced black olives and shredded basil leaves. Omit the salt.

Aubergine and Mint Dip Chop half a small aubergine (eggplant) and fry gently in olive oil until tender. Leave to cool. Fold into the dip omitting the mustard and add 45ml/3 tbsp chopped mint.

Saffron Dip

This herb and saffron dip is made with fromage frais for a light, refreshing texture. Substitute half the fromage frais for mayonnaise for a fuller flavour. Add more or less herbs depending on your taste.

SERVES FOUR

INGREDIENTS
  small pinch saffron threads
  200g/7oz/scant 1 cup fromage frais
  10 chives
  10 large basil leaves
  salt and ground black pepper

COOK'S TIP

Saffron has a unique flavour that cannot be substituted. Although expensive, a small pinch of the threads goes a long way, particularly if you chill the dip for a couple of hours before serving to let the flavours mingle.

Below: Herbs add subtle flavour and texture to dips.

1 Put 15ml/1 tbsp boiling water into a bowl and add the saffron threads. Leave to infuse (steep) for 5 minutes.

2 Beat the fromage frais in a large bowl until smooth. Stir in the infused saffron and liquid.

3 Chop the chives into the dip. Tear the basil leaves into small pieces and stir them in. Mix well. Season with salt and black pepper to taste. Transfer the saffron dip to a serving bowl, cover and refrigerate until ready to serve.

VARIATIONS
Ginger and Saffron Dip Finely grate (shred) a 2.5cm/1in length fresh root ginger. Stir into a little of the fromage frais, then add the rest. Add 30ml/2 tbsp chopped coriander (cilantro) instead of basil.
Apricot, Saffron and Almond Dip Finely chop 50g/2oz/¼ cup no-soak dried apricots and 40g/1½oz/⅓ cup lightly toasted flaked (sliced) almonds. Stir into the fromage frais with the saffron and add 15ml/1 tbsp chopped flat leaf parsley and 15ml/1 tbsp chopped coriander to the mixture instead of chives and basil.
Mascarpone and Rocket Dip Omit the saffron and make as above beating 115g/4oz/½ cup mascarpone into the fromage frais. Add a small handful of torn rocket (arugula) leaves (preferably wild rocket) with the herbs.
Saffron and Rosemary Dip Add 15ml/1 tbsp chopped rosemary to the saffron when infusing. Finish as above, substituting 15ml/1 tbsp grainy mustard and a handful of rosemary flowers, if available, for the chives and basil.
Parmesan and Sun-dried Tomato Dip Omit the saffron and add 25g/1oz/⅓ cup finely grated Parmesan cheese and 30ml/2 tbsp chopped sun-dried tomatoes from a jar.

HERB BUTTERS, CREAMS AND CHEESES

Dairy produce is subtle in flavour, and cream and butter in particular are often bland, making them ideal ingredients that will carry the flavour of aromatic herbs and spices.

FLAVOURED BUTTERS

A pat of herb butter, melting over steak, fish or vegetables, turns a fairly ordinary dish into something far more interesting. Almost any herbs can be used, the butters freeze well and have infinite uses: try them spread on to warm, crusty bread, scones (US biscuits) and sandwiches or swirled into soups and sauces.

Simple Herb Butters

To add interest to plain cooked meat, fish and vegetables, make a herb butter using a herb with a natural affinity to the main ingredient.

SERVES FOUR

INGREDIENTS
115g/4oz/½ cup softened butter
45ml/3 tbsp chopped herbs e.g.
parsley, thyme, rosemary, tarragon,
chives, basil, marjoram or coriander
(cilantro), or a mixture of several herbs
finely grated (shredded) rind of
½ lemon
good pinch cayenne pepper
salt and ground black pepper

1 Beat the butter until creamy, then beat in the herbs, lemon rind, cayenne and a little seasoning. Transfer to a small bowl and chill until required.

COOK'S TIP
Use herbs singly such as garlic, or make up a combination of herbs.

2 Alternatively, shape while still soft as follows:

Butter Slices Transfer the butter to a piece of greaseproof (waxed) paper and shape into a neat roll. Wrap and chill. Cut into slices.

Butter Shapes Put the butter on to a sheet of greaseproof paper and flatten to about 5mm/¼in thick with a palette knife (metal spatula). Chill and stamp out shapes using a cutter.

Below: Herb butter balls make a visually attractive accompaniment to food.

VARIATIONS
As well as being the traditional accompaniment to steaks, flavoured butters can be rubbed on to meat before roasting or spread over cutlets before barbecuing. They can be spread on fish that is foil-wrapped and baked in the oven, or used as you would garlic butter to make deliciously flavoured breads.

Anchovy and Tarragon Butter Omit the herbs. Add 4 drained and finely chopped canned anchovy fillets and 45ml/3 tbsp chopped tarragon.

Lavender and Thyme Butter Omit the herbs, cayenne pepper and seasoning and add 5 chopped lavender flowers and a small handful of thyme flowers.

Roasted Pepper Butter Halve 1 large red (bell) pepper and grill (broil), skin-side uppermost until blackened. Wrap in foil or plastic for 10 minutes then peel off the skins. Discard the stalk and seeds and finely chop the pepper. Allow to cool. Add to the butter with plenty of chopped basil, parsley or coriander (cilantro).

Mixed Flower Butter *(below)* For a special lunch or tea in the garden, a block of flower-adorned butter looks stunning. Gather plenty of sage, chive and rosemary flowers and sandwich some between two thick pats of chilled butter. Press more flowers around the sides of the butter. Cover and chill in the refrigerator.

HERB CREAMS AND CHEESES

Because of their intense, aromatic flavour, herbs are great for infusing in cream or milk to create some of the simplest dessert ideas. Infuse sweet herbs such as rosemary, bay, thyme, rose geranium and lavender in the milk or cream before making ice creams, custard and rice pudding, to add a fragrant depth to the finished dish. Sprigs of herbs make lovely garnishes.

Rosemary and Ratafia Cream

Make and chill this almond-flavoured cream in advance and serve with a platter of fresh summer fruits.

SERVES SIX

INGREDIENTS
300ml/½ pint/1¼ cups double
   (heavy) cream
several sprigs of rosemary
25g/1oz/½ cup ratafia biscuits
   (almond macaroons), crushed

Bring the cream slowly to the boil. Remove from the heat and add the rosemary. Leave to cool, then chill. Strain the cream into a bowl and whisk until it holds its shape. Fold in the biscuits and serve in a bowl. Chill.

VARIATIONS
Bay and Lemon Ratafia Cream Use 3 bay leaves instead of rosemary and add the finely grated (shredded) rind of 1 lemon when whisking.
Rose Geranium and Cointreau Cream Use 10 rose-geranium leaves instead of rosemary. Omit the biscuits. Add 15ml/1 tbsp Cointreau.

Above: Rosemary and ratafia-flavoured cream is ideal with summer berries.

HERB CREAMS

A platter of herb-flavoured cheeses makes a delicious finale to a light lunch. They also make delicious gifts. Use soft cheeses with a creamy consistency for best results. Store in a wrapping of waxed or baking parchment for up to 3 days.

Dill and Pink Peppercorn Cheese Finely chop several sprigs of dill and mix with 2.5ml/½ tsp crushed pink peppercorns. Using a teaspoon, spoon the mixture over the top and sides of a 150g/5oz medium-fat goat's cheese.
Thyme and Garlic Cheese Strip the leaves from several thyme stems adding any of the small flowers. Mix with a finely chopped garlic clove. Press the mixture over a 90g/3½oz round of full-fat goat's cheese.
Minted Feta Cheese Finely chop a small bunch of mint. Drain 200g/7oz feta cheese, cut into dice and roll in the mint until coated.
Tarragon and Lemon Cheese Cut a 200g/7oz pack of low-fat cream cheese into two. Tear the leaves off some tarragon and finely chop. Grate (shred) the rind of half a lemon. Mix with the tarragon and coat the cheese.

Below: Herb cheeses are delicious served with savoury biscuits or crackers.

HERB CONDIMENTS AND SUGARS

Flavouring salt, pepper, mustard and sugar with fresh herbs adds yet another dimension to their vast range of culinary uses. Many specialist shops and supermarkets stock a supply of ready-mixed herb and spice blends, but nothing can beat the fresh, vibrant flavour of home-made versions, a selection of which can add variety and interest to all aspects of cooking. The wealth of different herbs and spices around us provides plenty of scope for experimentation. This will inevitably lead to discovering some firm favourites which can be remade each season to take you through the winter.

Herby Salt

Allow time to dry the herbs before making herb salts.

MAKES ABOUT 300G/11OZ

INGREDIENTS
    6 dried bay leaves
    90ml/6 tbsp mixed dried herbs, such
        as thyme, rosemary, oregano,
        tarragon, dill, fennel
    300g/11oz coarse salt

1 Crumble all the herbs together in a large mortar. Add the salt and crush with a pestle until the herbs are finely distributed in the salt.

2 Transfer to an airtight container and store in a cool, dry place.

COOK'S TIP
Uses for Herby Salt
• Stir into tomato juice as an alternative to Tabasco or Worcester sauce.
• Rub into meat, poultry or fish as a dry marinade before roasting or grilling (broiling). Chill for an hour in the salt if you have time.
• Stir into soups, stews, casseroles and sauces.
• Sprinkle over chips and home-made crisps.
• Use as a seasoning for boiled eggs or quail's eggs.
• Use in salad dressings.

Right: Salt infused with herb layers.

Lemon Verbena Seasoning

This delicious blend of lemony flavours makes a wonderful dry marinade for chicken, lamb or pork.

MAKES ABOUT 50G/2OZ

INGREDIENTS
    2 lemons
    30ml/2 tbsp lemon thyme, chopped
    15ml/1 tbsp lemon verbena, chopped
    15ml/1 tbsp lemon grass, chopped

1 Pare fine strips of rind from the lemons, taking care not to remove too much of the white pith. Dry the rind and herbs on a rack in a warm place, such as an airing cupboard for 24–48 hours.

2 When thoroughly dry, pound the lemon rind using a mortar and pestle. Add the remaining ingredients and crush finely. Alternatively, use the small section of a food processor to blend the ingredients together.

3 Pack into small jars or fabric bags and store in a cool, dry place.

VARIATIONS
Herb Seasoning for Fish Use one or more of the following herbs: dill, parsley, chervil, tarragon and fennel, adding crushed dill or fennel seeds and lemon or ordinary pepper.
Herb Seasoning for Meat Use a mixture of rosemary, thyme, oregano, sage, parsley and chives, adding crushed black or white mustard seeds.
Lime and Herb Pepper Home-dried lime rind gives pepper extra bite and flavour. Finely grate (shred) the rind of 3 limes and leave to dry out on a tray for 24 hours. Grind with 115g/4oz black pepper and 60ml/4 tbsp dried rosemary, parsley or tarragon.
Spicy Salt Combine 15ml/1 tbsp each of cumin seeds, coriander seeds, black peppercorns and cardamom pods with a teaspoon each of ground cloves, chilli powder and ginger. Blend with the salt.

HERB MUSTARDS

Making mustard is surprisingly easy and produces really aromatic results. Use white mustard seeds for a mild flavour and the black seeds for extra heat.

Tarragon and Champagne Mustard

Enjoy this mustard, delicately flavoured with tarragon and champagne, with cold seafood or chicken.

MAKES ABOUT 250G/9OZ

INGREDIENTS
    30ml/2 tbsp mustard seeds
    75ml/5 tbsp champagne or white
        wine vinegar
    115g/4oz dry mustard powder
    115g/4oz/½ cup brown sugar
    2.5ml/½ tsp salt
    50ml/3½ tbsp olive oil
    60ml/4 tbsp chopped tarragon

1 Soak the mustard seeds overnight in the vinegar.

2 Pour the mixture into the bowl of a blender or small section of a food processor. Add the mustard powder, sugar and salt, and blend until smooth. Slowly add the oil while blending. Stir in the tarragon and pour into small, thoroughly clean jars. Store in a cool place for up to 6 weeks.

Horseradish Mustard

Traditionally associated with roast beef, fresh horseradish has a characteristically strong flavour with none of the taste of a store-bought brand. In this delicious recipe it blends with mustard to make a tangy relish for cold meats, smoked fish or cheese.

MAKES ABOUT 400G/14OZ

INGREDIENTS
    25g/1oz mustard seeds
    115g/4oz dry mustard powder
    115g/4oz/½ cup light muscovado
        (molasses) sugar
    120ml/4fl oz/½ cup white wine
        vinegar or cider vinegar
    50ml/2fl oz/¼ cup olive oil
    5ml/1 tsp lemon juice
    45ml/3 tbsp freshly grated
        (shredded) horseradish

1 Put the mustard seeds in a bowl and pour over 250ml/8fl oz/1 cup boiling water. Leave for 1 hour.

2 Drain the seeds, discarding the liquid, and place in a food processor or blender with the remaining ingredients. Blend until smooth.

3 Spoon into clean jars, and store in the refrigerator. Use fresh.

HERB, FLOWER AND SPICE SUGARS

The same technique that is used to flavour sugar with a vanilla pod (bean) works equally well with herbs, flowers and spices. Rose petals, rose-geranium leaves, lavender sprigs, cloves, cinnamon, ginger, cardamom and dried orange and lemon peel all make delicious flavourings, used either individually or in simple combinations. Once infused (steeped) for two weeks they can be used as a ready-made flavouring for creamy desserts, fruit salads, ice creams and custards, or sprinkled on to sponge cakes and pastries.

Making Infused Sugars

Ensure that flower petals are clean and dry, and break larger spices, such as cinnamon sticks, into smaller pieces. Layer up in small jars with caster (superfine) or granulated sugar and store in a cool, dry place. The greater the ratio of flavourings to sugar the more intense the final result.

Do not combine more than two or three different flavourings in each sugar or they might detract from each other. Combinations like rose petal, cardamom and ginger, or lavender and orange blend really well.

Below: Many aromatic ingredients can be used to infuse flavour.

HERBAL AND FLORAL DECORATIONS

Herbs and their romantic petite flowers can be used to make some of the prettiest culinary decorations. Crystallizing edible flowers – coating them in a fine dusting of caster (superfine) sugar – both enhances their delicate flavours and makes a simple and effective way of preserving them for later use. Once dry they can be stored in an airtight container for up to a week, ready to decorate special occasion cakes and summer desserts.

Freezing fresh herb flowers in ice cubes also prolongs the enjoyment of these stunning flowers, but most impressive of all is a classic "ice-bowl".

COOK'S TIPS
• Use any herb flowers or edible flowers such as mint, sweet cicely, sage, pansy, nasturtium, marigold, viola, rosemary, lavender, borage and rosebuds or small roses. Large roses can be used if separated into petals. You can use a mixture of colours but sometimes the bowls look more delicate if just one colour is used.
• Do not pack in too many herbs and flowers or the bowl will lose its clear icy look.
• Do not worry if you hear ice-cracking sounds when releasing the ice bowl. It will not fall apart!
• Do not be tempted to leave the bowls in hot water for too long as the ice will quickly melt and become fragile. Be cautious, even if it means redipping the bowl once or twice.
• For convenience, fill the bowl with ice cream or sorbet and return to the freezer so that it is ready and waiting for you. Serve on a plate, preferably glass, with a shallow rim to catch the melting ice.
• For a special occasion, ice bowls also look stunning filled with chilled water and floating candles.

Right: Ice bowls will retain their shape for many hours before melting, although keep out of the sun where possible. For a colour co-ordinated centrepiece, why not choose herbs and flowers that complement the taste or colours of the intended contents?

Herb-flower Ice Bowl

Easy to make, this stunning flower ice bowl provides a perfect container for ice creams and sorbets.

MAKES ONE BOWL

INGREDIENTS
  ice cubes
  freshly picked herb sprigs and their
    flowers (see Cook's Tips)
  freshly picked flowers
  water

1 Find two bowls, either glass or plastic, which will fit inside one another leaving a gap of about 2cm/¾in between them. Put some ice cubes in the base of the larger bowl and tuck some herb sprigs and flowers around them.

2 Position the smaller bowl inside it and tape the bowls together across the tops so that the smaller bowl is centred. Pour cold water into the large bowl until the level starts to come up the sides. Freeze for 2–3 hours until firm.

3 Tuck more herb sprigs and flowers between the two bowls using a skewer to arrange them so that they look attractive through the sides of the bowl. Fill the large bowl with water until it comes to the rim. Carefully transfer to the freezer and freeze overnight.

4 Peel off the tape. Half-fill a washing-up bowl with hot water, sit the frozen bowls in it and pour a little hot water into the smaller bowl. Count to 30 then remove the bowls and pour the water out of the small bowl. Use a thin knife to loosen the ice from the edges of the bowls.

Making Floral Ice Cubes

Use small herb flowers that will tuck easily into ice-cube compartments, or separate larger flowers into petals. Small summer fruits such as red and white currants or raspberries can be tucked in with the flowers. Use the ice cubes in punches, cordials, sparkling table water or to decorate a platter of summer fruits.

INGREDIENTS
  a selection of freshly picked edible
    flowers
  cold water

1 Pour water into ice-cube trays until they are half full.

2 Position the flowers using tweezers, if easier to handle. Freeze for about 1 hour, or until firm. Add more water to fill the trays and refreeze until firm.

Below: Floral ice cubes make an attractive addition to a glass of summer punch or herb-flavoured cordial.

Crystallized Flowers

Pick flowers for crystallization when they are perfectly dry, and check that they are free of insects. Most herb flowers can be crystallized (candied), although some, like rosemary and thyme flowers are too fiddly to bother with. Borage, sage, nasturtium, sweet cicely fronds and rose petals work really well, as do other edible flowers like violas, violets, pansies, primroses, cowslips and pinks.

INGREDIENTS
  1 egg white
  caster (superfine) sugar
  plenty of fresh flowers or petals

1 Put the egg white into a small bowl and lightly whisk until it is broken up.

2 Coat a flower with egg white, using a paintbrush. Sprinkle the flower with sugar and shake off the excess. Transfer to a sheet of baking parchment and leave in a warm place until dry. Store in a sealed container for up to a week until ready to use.

COOK'S TIP

If you want the crystallized flowers to keep for more than a week it is best to use gum arabic (available from a chemist) instead of egg white. Dissolve 5ml/1 tsp in 25ml/ 1½ tbsp water or a colourless spirit such as gin or vodka and follow the recipe for the remaining steps. Gum arabic will make the petals very hard and brittle, so keep in a cool place away from any source of moisture.

Crystallized Roses

Coat all the petals in egg white and sugar as before, then push one end of a 15cm/6in length of fine floristry wire through the flower base. Bend and hook the other end of the wire over the rim of a tall glass or bowl so the rose is suspended. Leave until dry.

Below: Fresh roses dusted with sugar are stylish and sophisticated and deceptively simple to make.

SPRING

Spring brings a breath of fresh air, and the taste of fresh herbs. Banish the winter blues, along with all those hearty casseroles and stews, with lighter, delicately flavoured, aromatic dishes that will wake up the taste buds, enliven the spirits and invigorate the system. Make the most of herbs that cannot be dried successfully, but which are now available fresh. Basil, chervil, dill, mint and tarragon are all bursting into growth and the sight  and scent of tender green lovage will gladden the cook's heart. Lots of these herbs are the perfect partners for fish, a favourite choice for spring dishes, and superb with baby vegetables, while who could resist the new season's lamb coated in a fresh herb crust? This is the time to give herbs a starring role, as a topping for pizza, the main flavouring for soup or a tasty partner for pasta.

 Although onions and garlic have been available all winter, and are rightly prized for their flavour, the new season's crop of fresh chives brings a deliciously different, fresh taste to salads, dips and all kinds of sauces. Try them in Seared Scallops with Chive Sauce on Leek and Carrot Rice, or the aromatic Garlic and Chive Risotto with Frizzled Onions and Parmesan.

Now is the time to be lavish with herbs and use them for attractive and appetizing garnishes. Coriander (cilantro) and flat leaf parsley, both flourishing at this time of year, always look pretty on a serving platter, and while chopped chives are an easy garnish, they can also be tied together in little bundles for a more effective decoration. Delicate fronds of dill or a simple sprinkling of fresh basil or sage leaves add a final touch to many dishes.

From risotto to home-made bread and from seafood to poultry, fresh herbs feature – subtly or extravagantly – in recipes guaranteed to put a spring in your step.

GARLIC AND CORIANDER SOUP

THIS RECIPE IS BASED ON THE WONDERFUL BREAD SOUPS OR ACORDAS OF PORTUGAL. USING THE BEST-QUALITY INGREDIENTS WILL ENSURE THIS SIMPLE SOUP IS A SUCCESS.

SERVES SIX

INGREDIENTS
   25g/1oz/1 cup fresh coriander
      (cilantro), leaves and stalks
      chopped separately
   1.5 litres/2½ pints/6¼ cups
      vegetable or chicken stock, or water
   5–6 plump garlic cloves, peeled
   6 eggs
   275g/10oz day-old bread, with most
      of the crust removed, torn into
      bitesize pieces
   90ml/6 tbsp extra virgin olive oil,
      plus extra to serve
   salt and ground black pepper

1 Place the coriander stalks in a pan. Add the stock or water and bring to the boil. Lower the heat and simmer for 10 minutes, then process in a food processor or blender. Sieve the soup and return it to the pan.

2 Crush the garlic with 5ml/1 tsp salt, then stir in 120ml/4fl oz/½ cup of the hot soup. Return the mixture to the rest of the soup in the pan.

3 Meanwhile, poach the eggs in a frying pan of simmering water for 3–4 minutes, or until just set. Use a draining spoon to remove them from the pan and transfer to a warmed plate. Trim off any untidy bits of white.

4 Meanwhile, bring the soup back to the boil and add seasoning to taste. Stir in the chopped coriander leaves and remove from the heat.

5 Place the bread in six soup plates or bowls and drizzle the oil over it. Ladle in the soup and stir. Add a poached egg to each bowl and serve immediately, offering olive oil at the table so that it can be drizzled over the soup as desired.

ROASTED GARLIC TOASTS

GARLIC ROASTED OR BARBECUED IN ITS SKIN BECOMES A SOFT, AROMATIC PURÉE WITH A SWEET, NUTTY FLAVOUR, WHICH IS PERFECTLY COMPLEMENTED BY AROMATIC ROSEMARY. SPREAD ON CRISP TOAST TO MAKE A DELICIOUS STARTER OR ACCOMPANIMENT TO MEAT OR VEGETABLE DISHES.

<u>SERVES FOUR</u>

INGREDIENTS
2 whole garlic heads
extra virgin olive oil, for brushing
and drizzling
fresh rosemary sprigs
ciabatta loaf or thick baguette
chopped fresh rosemary
salt and ground black pepper

4 Slice the ciabatta or baguette and brush each slice generously with olive oil. Toast the slices until they are crisp and golden, turning once.

5 Squeeze the garlic cloves from their skins on to the toasts. Sprinkle with the chopped fresh rosemary and olive oil, and add salt and black pepper to taste.

1 Preheat the oven to 200°C/400°F/ Gas 6 or light the barbecue, if using. Remove the tops from both of the whole heads of garlic, by slicing them with a sharp kitchen knife.

2 Brush the garlic heads with extra virgin olive oil and add a few sprigs of fresh rosemary, before wrapping in kitchen foil.

3 Bake the foil parcels in the oven for 25–30 minutes, or until the garlic is soft. Alternatively, cook the parcels on a medium-hot barbecue, turning them over occasionally.

PASTA SALAD WITH PRAWNS AND HERBS

THIS PRAWN AND PASTA SALAD IS ENLIVENED WITH A LEMON, BASIL AND CORIANDER DRESSING, SPIKED WITH A LITTLE RED CHILLI. IT MAKES AN ATTRACTIVE AND DELICIOUS LUNCH SERVED WITH WARM CIABATTA BREAD.

SERVES FOUR

INGREDIENTS
    225g/8oz/2 cups dried farfalle
    juice of ½ lemon
    1 small fresh red chilli, seeded and
      very finely chopped
    60ml/4 tbsp chopped fresh basil
    30ml/2 tbsp chopped fresh
      coriander (cilantro)
    60ml/4 tbsp extra virgin olive oil
    15ml/1 tbsp mayonnaise
    250g/9oz/1½ cups peeled cooked
      prawns (shrimp)
    1 avocado
    salt and ground black pepper

1 Cook the pasta in a large pan of boiling salted water until *al dente*.

2 Meanwhile, put the lemon juice and chilli in a bowl with half the basil and coriander, and salt and pepper to taste. Whisk well to mix, then whisk in the oil and mayonnaise until thick.

3 Add the prawns and gently stir to coat them with the dressing.

4 Drain the pasta into a colander, and rinse under cold running water until cold. Leave to drain and dry, shaking the colander occasionally.

5 Halve and peel the avocado, then cut the flesh into neat dice. Add to the prawns and dressing with the pasta, toss well to mix and taste for seasoning. Serve immediately, sprinkled with the remaining basil and coriander.

COOK'S TIP
This pasta salad can be made several hours ahead of time, without the avocado. Cover the bowl with clear film (plastic wrap) and chill. Prepare the avocado and add it to the salad just before serving, or it will discolour.

LINGUINE WITH ROCKET

THIS IS A FIRST COURSE THAT YOU WILL FIND IN MANY A FASHIONABLE RESTAURANT IN ITALY. THE DISTINCTIVE PEPPERY FLAVOUR OF ROCKET IS WELL DEFINED IN THIS QUICK AND EASY-TO-PREPARE DISH, WHICH COULD ALSO BE MADE WITH SPAGHETTI.

SERVES FOUR

INGREDIENTS
  350g/12oz fresh or dried linguine
  120ml/4fl oz/½ cup extra virgin olive oil
  150g/5oz rocket (arugula)
  75g/3oz/1 cup freshly grated
    (shredded) Parmesan cheese
  salt and ground black pepper

1 Cook the pasta in a large pan of boiling salted water, then drain.

2 Heat about 60ml/4 tbsp of the olive oil in the pasta pan, then add the drained pasta, then the rocket. Toss over a medium to high heat for 1–2 minutes or until the rocket is just wilted, then remove from the heat.

3 Tip the pasta and rocket into a warmed large bowl. Add half the freshly grated Parmesan and the remaining olive oil. Add a little salt and black pepper to taste.

4 Toss the mixture quickly to mix. Serve immediately, sprinkled with the remaining Parmesan.

COOK'S TIP
Buy rocket by the bunch from the greengrocer. The type sold in small cellophane packets in supermarkets is very expensive for this kind of dish. Always check when buying rocket that all the leaves are bright green. In hot weather, rocket quickly turns yellow.

Seared Scallops with Chive Sauce on Leek and Carrot Rice

The sweet flesh of scallops pairs superbly with the delicate flavour of chives. Served on a bed of wild and white rice with leeks, carrots and chervil, this is an impressive dish.

SERVES FOUR

INGREDIENTS
    12–16 shelled scallops
    45ml/3 tbsp olive oil
    50g/2oz/⅓ cup wild rice
    65g/2½oz/5 tbsp butter
    4 carrots, cut into long, thin strips
    2 leeks, cut into thick diagonal slices
    1 small onion, finely chopped
    90g/3½oz/½ cup long grain rice
    1 fresh bay leaf
    200ml/7fl oz/scant 1 cup white wine
    450ml/¾ pint/scant 2 cups well-
       flavoured fish stock
    60ml/4 tbsp double (heavy) cream
    a little lemon juice
    25ml/1½ tbsp chopped fresh chives
    30ml/2 tbsp chopped fresh chervil
    salt and ground black pepper

1 Lightly season the scallops, brush with 15ml/1 tbsp of the olive oil and set aside.

2 Cook the wild rice in plenty of boiling water for about 30 minutes, until tender, then drain.

3 Melt half the butter in a small frying pan and sauté the carrots fairly gently for 4–5 minutes. Add the leeks and fry for another 2 minutes.

4 Season to taste and add 30–45ml/ 2–3 tbsp water, then cover and cook for a few minutes. Uncover and cook until the liquid evaporates. Set aside off the heat.

5 Melt half the rest of the butter with 15ml/1 tbsp of the remaining oil in a heavy pan. Add the onion and fry for 3–4 minutes, or until softened but not browned.

6 Add the long grain rice and bay leaf and cook, stirring constantly, until the rice looks translucent and the grains are coated with oil.

7 Pour in half the wine and half the stock. Season with 2.5ml/½ tsp salt and bring to the boil. Stir, then cover and cook very gently for 15 minutes, or until the liquid is absorbed and the rice is cooked and tender.

8 Reheat the carrots and leeks gently, then stir them into the long grain rice with the wild rice. Add seasoning to taste, if necessary.

9 Meanwhile, pour the remaining wine and stock into a small pan and boil rapidly until the liquid has reduced by about half.

COOK'S TIP
To shell a fresh scallop, hold it firmly with the flat-side up, and insert a strong knife blade between the shells to cut the top muscle. Separate the two shells. Slide the knife blade under the skirt to cut the second muscle. Remove the scallop. The edible part is the round white part and the coral, or roe, if present. Discard the beard-like fringe and intestinal thread.

10 Heat a heavy frying pan over a high heat. Add the remaining butter and olive oil. Sear the scallops for 1–2 minutes each side, or until browned, then remove and keep warm.

11 Pour the reduced stock into the frying pan and heat until bubbling, then add the double cream and boil until the mixture is thickened. Season with lemon juice, salt and black pepper. Stir in the chopped chives.

12 Stir the chervil into the rice and vegetable mixture and pile it on to plates. Arrange the scallops on top and spoon the sauce over the rice.

SALMON RISOTTO WITH CUCUMBER AND TARRAGON

THE SUBTLE FLAVOUR OF CUCUMBER IS A FAMILIAR COMPANION FOR SALMON. IN THIS SIMPLE RISOTTO FRESH TARRAGON ADDS ITS UNMISTAKABLE, DELICATE AROMA AND FLAVOUR.

SERVES FOUR

INGREDIENTS
  25g/1oz/2 tbsp butter
  small bunch of spring onions
    (scallions), white parts only,
    chopped
  ½ cucumber, peeled, seeded
    and chopped
  350g/12oz/1¾ cups risotto rice
  1.2 litres/2 pints/5 cups hot chicken
    or fish stock
  150ml/¼ pint/⅔ cup dry white wine
  450g/1lb salmon fillet, skinned
    and diced
  45ml/3 tbsp chopped fresh tarragon
  salt and ground black pepper

1 Heat the butter in a large pan and add the spring onions and cucumber. Cook for 2–3 minutes, stirring occasionally. Do not let the spring onions colour.

2 Stir in the risotto rice, then pour in the stock and white wine. Bring to the boil, then lower the heat and allow to simmer, uncovered, for 10 minutes, stirring occasionally.

3 Stir in the diced salmon and then season to taste with salt and ground black pepper. Continue cooking for a further 5 minutes, stirring occasionally to avoid sticking, then remove from the heat. Cover the pan and leave the risotto to stand for 5 minutes.

4 Remove the lid, add the chopped fresh tarragon and mix lightly. Spoon the risotto into a warmed bowl and serve immediately.

COOK'S TIP
Carnaroli risotto rice would be an excellent choice for this risotto, although, if it is not available, arborio rice can be used instead.

HERB-CRUSTED RACK OF LAMB WITH PUY LENTILS

THIS ROAST IS QUICK AND EASY TO PREPARE, YET IMPRESSIVE WHEN SERVED: THE PERFECT CHOICE WHEN ENTERTAINING. BOILED OR STEAMED NEW POTATOES AND LIGHTLY COOKED BROCCOLI OR SUGAR SNAP PEAS ARE SUITABLE ACCOMPANIMENTS FOR THE LAMB. SERVE WITH A LIGHT RED WINE.

SERVES FOUR

INGREDIENTS
   2 x 6-bone racks of lamb, chined
   50g/2oz/1 cup fresh white
     breadcrumbs
   2 large garlic cloves, crushed
   90ml/6 tbsp chopped mixed fresh
     herbs, such as rosemary, thyme, flat
     leaf parsley and marjoram, plus
     extra sprigs to garnish
   50g/2oz ¼ cup butter, melted
   salt and ground black pepper
For the Puy lentils
   1 red onion, chopped
   30ml/2 tbsp olive oil
   400g/14oz can Puy or green lentils,
     rinsed and drained
   400g/14oz can chopped tomatoes
   30ml/2 tbsp chopped fresh parsley

1 Preheat the oven to 220°C/425°F/ Gas 7. Trim any excess fat from the lamb, season and place in a roasting tin.

2 Mix together the breadcrumbs, garlic, chopped herbs and butter. Press the mixture on to the fat-sides of the lamb. Roast for 25 minutes. Cover with foil and stand for 5 minutes before carving.

3 Cook the onion in the olive oil until softened. Add the lentils and tomatoes and cook gently for 5 minutes, or until the lentils are piping hot. Stir in the parsley and season to taste.

4 Cut each rack of lamb in half and serve with the lentils and new potatoes. Garnish with herb sprigs.

TURKEY ESCALOPES WITH LEMON AND SAGE

SAGE IS A USEFUL HERB THAT CAN BE HARVESTED ALL THE YEAR ROUND. ITS WELL-DEFINED FLAVOUR BLENDS PERFECTLY WITH LEMON IN A MARINADE FOR TURKEY ESCALOPES USED HERE.

2 In a small bowl, combine the lemon rind, sage, lemon juice, and 30ml/ 2 tbsp of the oil. Stir well to mix.

3 Arrange the turkey cutlets, in one layer, in one or two shallow baking dishes. Divide the lemon mixture evenly between the dishes and rub well into the turkey. Leave to marinate for 20 minutes.

4 Heat the remaining oil in a frying pan. Dredge the turkey cutlets in the breadcrumbs, shaking off the excess.

5 Fry in the hot oil for about 2 minutes on each side. Garnish with sage leaves and lemon slices, and serve with courgettes and new potatoes.

SERVES FOUR

INGREDIENTS

- 4 turkey cutlets (boneless slices of breast, about 175g/6oz each)
- 15ml/1 tbsp freshly grated (shredded) lemon rind
- 15ml/1 tbsp chopped fresh sage or 5ml/1 tsp dried sage
- 50ml/2fl oz/¼ cup fresh lemon juice
- 90ml/6 tbsp vegetable oil
- 50g/2oz/scant 1 cup fine dry breadcrumbs
- salt and ground black pepper
- fresh sage leaves and lemon slices, to garnish
- steamed courgettes (zucchini) and new potatoes, to serve

1 Place each turkey cutlet between two sheets of greaseproof (waxed) paper or clear film. With the flat side of a meat mallet, pound until about 5mm/¼in thick, being careful not to split the meat. Remove the paper or clear film. Sprinkle the cutlets with salt and pepper.

VARIATION
For an equally delicious alternative, substitute fresh tarragon leaves for the sage used here.

CHICKEN WITH FORTY CLOVES OF GARLIC

THIS DISH DOES NOT HAVE TO BE MATHEMATICALLY EXACT — THE IMPORTANT THING IS THAT THERE SHOULD BE LOTS OF GARLIC. THE SMELL THAT EMANATES FROM THE OVEN AS THE CHICKEN AND GARLIC COOK IS INDESCRIBABLY DELICIOUS.

SERVES FOUR TO FIVE

INGREDIENTS
- 5–6 whole heads of garlic
- 15g/½oz/1 tbsp butter
- 45ml/3 tbsp olive oil
- 1.8–2kg/4–4½lb chicken
- 150g/5oz/1¼ cups plain (all-purpose) flour, plus 5ml/1 tsp
- 75ml/5 tbsp white port, Pineau de Charentes or other white, fortified wine
- 2–3 fresh tarragon or rosemary sprigs
- 30ml/2 tbsp crème fraîche (optional)
- few drops of lemon juice (optional)
- salt and ground black pepper

1 Separate three of the heads of garlic into cloves and peel them. Remove the first layer of papery skin from the remaining heads of garlic and cut off the tops to expose the cloves, but leave them whole. Preheat the oven to 180°C/350°F/Gas 4.

2 Heat the butter and 15ml/1 tbsp of the olive oil in a flameproof casserole which is just large enough to take the chicken and garlic. Add the chicken and cook over a medium heat, turning frequently, for 10–15 minutes, or until it is browned all over.

3 Sprinkle in 5ml/1 tsp flour and cook for 1 minute. Add the port or wine. Tuck in the whole heads of garlic and the peeled cloves with the herb sprigs. Pour over the remaining oil and season to taste with salt and pepper.

4 Mix the main batch of flour with sufficient water to make a firm dough. Roll it out into a long sausage and press it around the rim of the casserole, then press on the lid, folding the dough up and over the lid to create a tight seal. Cook in the oven for 1½ hours.

5 To serve, break the seal and remove the chicken and whole garlic to a serving platter and keep warm.

6 Remove and discard the herb sprigs, then place the casserole on the hob and whisk the contents to combine the garlic with the juices. Add the crème fraîche, if using, and a little lemon juice to taste, if liked. Process the sauce in a food processor or blender or press it through a sieve if a smoother result is required. Serve the garlic purée with the chicken.

RICE WITH DILL AND BROAD BEANS

THIS IS A FAVOURITE RICE DISH IN IRAN, WHERE IT IS CALLED BAGHALI POLO. THE COMBINATION OF BROAD BEANS, DILL, WARM CINNAMON AND CUMIN WORKS VERY WELL. THE SAFFRON RICE ADDS A SPLASH OF BRIGHT COLOUR.

SERVES FOUR

INGREDIENTS

275g/10oz/1½ cups basmati
  rice, soaked
750ml/1¼ pints/3 cups water
40g/1½oz/3 tbsp butter
175g/6oz/1½ cups frozen baby broad
  (fava) beans, thawed and peeled
90ml/6 tbsp finely chopped fresh
  dill, plus 1 fresh dill sprig,
  to garnish
5ml/1 tsp ground cinnamon
5ml/1 tsp ground cumin
2–3 saffron threads, soaked in
  15ml/1 tbsp boiling water
salt

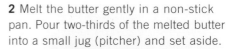

1 Drain the rice, tip it into a pan and pour in the water. Add a little salt. Bring to the boil, then lower the heat and simmer very gently for 5 minutes. Drain, rinse well in warm water and then drain once again.

2 Melt the butter gently in a non-stick pan. Pour two-thirds of the melted butter into a small jug (pitcher) and set aside.

3 Spoon enough rice into the pan to cover the base. Add a quarter of the beans and a little dill. Spread over another layer of rice, then a layer of beans and dill. Repeat the layers until all the beans and dill have been used up, ending with a layer of rice. Cook over a gentle heat for 8 minutes until the rice and beans are nearly tender.

4 Pour the reserved melted butter over the rice. Sprinkle with the ground cinnamon and cumin. Cover the pan with a clean dish towel and a tight-fitting lid, lifting the corners of the cloth back over the lid. Cook over a low heat for 25–30 minutes.

5 Spoon about 45ml/3 tbsp of the cooked rice into the bowl of saffron water; mix well. Mound the remaining rice mixture on a large serving plate and spoon the saffron rice on one side to decorate. Serve at once, decorated with the sprig of dill.

SESAME-SEED-COATED FALAFEL WITH TAHINI AND MINT YOGURT DIP

THESE SPICY PATTIES HAVE A CRUNCHY COATING OF SESAME SEEDS. SERVE WITH THE MINT-FLAVOURED TAHINI YOGURT DIP AND WARM PITTA BREAD AS A LIGHT LUNCH OR SUPPER DISH.

SERVES FOUR

INGREDIENTS
250g/9oz/1⅓ cups dried chickpeas
2 garlic cloves, crushed
1 red chilli, seeded and finely sliced
5ml/1 tsp ground coriander seeds
5ml/1 tsp ground cumin
15ml/1 tbsp chopped fresh mint
15ml/1 tbsp chopped fresh parsley
2 spring onions (scallions), finely
  chopped
1 large egg, beaten
sesame seeds, for coating
sunflower oil, for frying
salt and ground black pepper
For the tahini yogurt dip
30ml/2 tbsp light tahini
200g/7oz/scant 1 cup natural
  (plain) yogurt
5ml/1 tsp cayenne pepper, plus extra
  for sprinkling
15ml/1 tbsp chopped fresh mint
1 spring onion (scallion),
  finely sliced

3 Combine the chickpeas with the garlic, chilli, ground spices, herbs, spring onions and seasoning, then mix in the egg. Place in a food processor and blend until the mixture forms a coarse paste. If the paste seems too soft, chill it for 30 minutes.

4 Form the chilled chickpea paste into 12 patties with your hands, then roll in the sesame seeds to coat thoroughly.

1 Place the chickpeas in a bowl, cover with cold water and leave to soak overnight. Drain and rinse them, then place in a pan and cover with cold water. Bring to the boil and boil rapidly for 10 minutes, reduce the heat and simmer for 1½–2 hours. Drain.

2 To make the tahini yogurt dip, mix together the tahini, yogurt, cayenne pepper and mint in a small bowl. Sprinkle the spring onion and extra cayenne on top, and chill until required.

GARLIC AND CHIVE RISOTTO WITH FRIZZLED ONIONS AND PARMESAN

GARLIC, ONIONS AND CHIVES BELONG TO THE ALLIUM FAMILY OF PLANTS. THE ONIONS ARE FIRST GENTLY COOKED IN BUTTER — AS IN ALL CLASSIC RISOTTOS — THEN GARLIC AND CHIVES ARE ADDED. THE RISOTTO IS TOPPED WITH A FINAL SPRINKLING OF DELICIOUS, CRISP FRIED ONIONS.

4 Continue cooking for 18–20 minutes, adding one or two ladlefuls of stock at a time, until the rice is swollen and tender outside, but still *al dente* on the inside. Keep the heat low and stir frequently. The finished risotto should be moist, but not like soup.

5 Separate the slices of yellow onion into rings while the risotto is cooking. Heat a shallow layer of oil in a frying pan. Cook the onion rings slowly at first until they are soft, then increase the heat and fry them briskly until they are brown and crisp. Drain them thoroughly on kitchen paper.

SERVES FOUR

INGREDIENTS
75g/3oz/6 tbsp butter
15ml/1 tbsp olive oil, plus extra for shallow frying
1 onion, finely chopped
4 garlic cloves, finely chopped
350g/12oz/1⅔ cups risotto rice
150ml/¼ pint/⅔ cup dry white wine
pinch of saffron threads (about 12 threads)
about 1.2 litres/2 pints/5 cups simmering vegetable stock
1 large yellow onion, thinly sliced
15g/½oz chopped fresh chives
75g/3oz/1 cup freshly grated (shredded) Parmesan cheese, plus extra to taste
salt and ground black pepper

1 Melt half the butter with the oil in a large, deep frying pan or heavy pan. Add the onion with a pinch of salt and cook over a very low heat, stirring frequently, for 10–15 minutes, or until softened and just turning golden. Do not allow the onion to brown.

2 Add the garlic and rice and cook, stirring constantly, for 3–4 minutes, or until the rice is coated and looks translucent. Season with a little salt and ground black pepper.

3 Pour in the wine and stir in the saffron with a ladleful of hot stock. Cook slowly, stirring frequently, until all the liquid has been absorbed.

6 Beat the chopped chives, the remaining butter and half the Parmesan into the risotto until it looks creamy. Taste and add salt and ground black pepper, if necessary.

7 Serve the risotto in warmed bowls, topped with the crisp fried onions. Add more grated Parmesan to taste at the table.

FRESH HERB PIZZA

WONDERFUL FRESH SUMMER HERBS COMBINE WITH CREAM AND GARLIC IN THIS HEAVENLY PIZZA.
SERVE WITH A CRISP GREEN SALAD WITH PLENTY OF DRESSING

SERVES EIGHT

INGREDIENTS

   115g/4oz/4 cups mixed fresh herbs,
    such as parsley, basil and oregano
   3 garlic cloves, crushed
   120ml/4fl oz/½ cup double
    (heavy) cream
   1 pizza base, 25–30cm/10–12in
    diameter
   15ml/1 tbsp garlic oil
   115g/4oz/1 cup grated Pecorino
    cheese
   salt and ground black pepper

1 Preheat the oven to 220°C/425°F/
Gas 7. Chop the herbs, in a food
processor if you have one.

2 In a bowl mix together the herbs,
garlic, cream and seasoning.

3 Brush the pizza base with the garlic
oil, then spread over the herb mixture.

4 Sprinkle over the Pecorino. Bake for
15–20 minutes, or until crisp and
golden and the topping is still moist.
Cut into thin wedges and serve
immediately.

ONION, THYME AND OLIVE BREAD

THIS BREAD IS DELICIOUSLY FLAVOURED WITH BLACK OLIVES, ONION AND THYME, AND IS GOOD FOR SANDWICHES OR CUT INTO THICK SLICES AND DIPPED IN OLIVE OIL. IT IS ALSO EXCELLENT TOASTED, MAKING A WONDERFUL BASE FOR BRUSCHETTA OR DELICIOUS CROÛTONS FOR TOSSING INTO SALAD.

**MAKES ONE LARGE OR
TWO SMALL LOAVES**

INGREDIENTS
  350g/12oz/3 cups unbleached
    strong white bread flour, plus
    extra for dusting
  115g/4oz/1 cup corn meal, plus a
    little extra
  rounded 5ml/1 tsp salt
  15g/½oz fresh yeast or 10ml/2 tsp
    dried yeast
  5ml/1 tsp muscovado (molasses)
    sugar
  warm water
  15ml/1 tbsp chopped fresh thyme
  30ml/2 tbsp olive oil, plus extra
    for greasing
  1 red onion, finely chopped
  75g/3oz/1 cup freshly grated
    (shredded) Parmesan cheese
  90g/3½oz/scant 1 cup pitted black
    olives, halved

2 Make a well in the centre of the dry ingredients and pour in the yeast liquid and a further 150ml/¼ pint/⅔ cup of warm water.

3 Add the chopped thyme and 15ml/1 tbsp of the olive oil and mix thoroughly with a wooden spoon, gradually drawing in the dry ingredients until they are fully incorporated. Add a dash more warm water, if necessary, to make a soft, but not sticky, dough.

4 Knead the dough on a lightly floured work surface for 5 minutes, or until it is smooth and elastic.

5 Place in a clean, lightly oiled bowl and then place in a plastic bag or cover with oiled clear film. Set aside to rise in a warm, but not hot, place for 1–2 hours, or until well risen.

7 Brush a baking sheet with olive oil. Turn out the risen dough on to a floured work surface. Gently knead in the cooked onions, followed by the freshly grated Parmesan cheese and, finally, the halved black olives.

8 Shape the dough into one or two oval loaves. Sprinkle the extra corn meal on to the work surface and roll the bread in it, then place the loaf or loaves on the prepared baking sheet.

1 Mix the flour, corn meal and salt in a warmed bowl. If using fresh yeast, cream it with the sugar and gradually stir in 120ml/4fl oz/½ cup of the warm water. If using dried yeast, stir the sugar into the water and sprinkle the dried yeast over the surface. Leave in a warm place for 10 minutes, or until frothy.

6 Meanwhile, heat the remaining olive oil in a large, heavy frying pan. Add the chopped onion and cook over a fairly gentle heat, stirring occasionally, for about 8 minutes, or until the onion has turned soft and golden, but is not at all browned. Set aside to cool.

9 Make several criss-cross lines across the top of the loaf or loaves. Slip the baking sheet into the plastic bag, or cover with a layer of oiled clear film and leave to rise once again in a warm place for about 1 hour, or until well risen. Preheat the oven to 200°C/400°F/Gas 6.

COOK'S TIP
The best type of Parmesan is Parmigiano reggiano, which is made in the Reggio Emilia area of Italy. It will keep for several weeks in the refrigerator, wrapped in foil.

VARIATION
If you prefer, shape the dough into a loaf, roll in corn meal and place in a lightly oiled loaf tin (pan). Leave to rise, as in step 9, until risen well above the rim of the tin. Bake for 35–40 minutes, or until it sounds hollow when turned out and tapped on the base.

10 Bake the loaf or loaves for 30–35 minutes, or until the bread sounds hollow when tapped on the base. Leave to cool on a wire rack.

CURD TARTS WITH LEMON AND COINTREAU

LEMON EMPHASIZES THE ORANGE AND COINTREAU FILLING, AND A LITTLE NUTMEG ADDS A WARM AND SPICY TOUCH TO THESE TRADITIONAL ENGLISH TARTS. EXCELLENT SERVED WITH HOME-MADE CUSTARD.

SERVES SIX

INGREDIENTS
175g/6oz/1½ cups plain (all-purpose) flour, plus extra for dusting
40g/1½oz/3 tbsp block margarine, diced
40g/1½oz/3 tbsp white vegetable fat (shortening), diced
30ml/2 tbsp caster (superfine) sugar
1 egg yolk
2.5ml/½ tsp ground nutmeg
orange segments and thinly pared orange rind, to decorate
For the filling
25g/1oz/2 tbsp butter, melted
50g/2oz/¼ cup caster (superfine) sugar
1 egg
175g/6oz/¾ cup curd (farmer's) cheese
30ml/2 tbsp double (heavy) cream
50g/2oz/¼ cup currants
15ml/1 tbsp grated (shredded) lemon rind
15ml/1 tbsp grated (shredded) orange rind
15ml/1 tbsp Cointreau

1 Start by making the pastry. Sift the flour into a large mixing bowl and rub in the margarine and vegetable fat until the mixture resembles fine breadcrumbs. Stir in the sugar and egg yolk and then add enough cold water to make a firm dough.

2 Wrap the pastry in clear film and chill for 30 minutes. Preheat the oven to 190°C/375°F/Gas 5.

COOK'S TIPS

• Curd cheese is a soft, unripened cheese with a milky, tangy flavour. If it is not available, cottage cheese can be used instead, although it will not have the same tang. Process in a food processor or press through a sieve, then use as curd cheese.
• To make a large tart, use the pastry to line an 18cm/7in flan tin (quiche pan). Spoon in the filling and bake at the same temperature for 45–55 minutes.

3 Roll out the dough on a lightly floured surface and use it to line six 10cm/4in fluted flan tins (tart pans).

4 To make the filling, combine the melted butter, sugar, egg, curd cheese, cream, currants, grated lemon and orange rinds and Cointreau in a bowl. Mix well. Spoon the mixture into the pastry cases and smooth out, sprinkle over the nutmeg and bake for 30–35 minutes. Serve decorated with orange segments and the pared orange rind.

RICH LEMON POPPY-SEED CAKE

THE CLASSIC COMBINATION OF POPPY SEEDS AND LEMON IS USED FOR THIS LIGHT CAKE, WHICH HAS A DELICIOUS LEMON CURD AND FROMAGE FRAIS FILLING.

<u>SERVES EIGHT</u>

INGREDIENTS
- 350g/12oz/1½ cups unsalted (sweet) butter, plus extra for greasing
- 350g/12oz/1¾ cups golden caster (superfine) sugar
- 45ml/3 tbsp poppy seeds
- 20ml/4 tsp finely grated (shredded) lemon rind
- 70ml/4½ tbsp luxury lemon curd
- 6 eggs, separated
- 120ml/4fl oz/½ cup semi-skimmed (low-fat) milk
- 350g/12oz/3 cups unbleached self-raising (self-rising) flour, plus extra for dusting
- icing (confectioners') sugar, to decorate

For the filling
- 150g/5oz/½ cup luxury lemon curd
- 150ml/¼ pint/⅔ cup fromage frais

1 Butter and lightly flour two 23cm/9in springform cake tins (pans). Preheat the oven to 180°C/350°F/Gas 4.

2 Cream the butter and sugar until light and fluffy. Add the poppy seeds, lemon rind, lemon curd and egg yolks and beat well, then add the milk and mix well. Fold in the flour until combined.

3 Whisk the egg whites using a hand-held electric mixer until they form soft peaks. Carefully fold the egg whites into the cake mixture until just combined. Divide between the prepared tins.

4 Bake for 40–45 minutes, or until a skewer inserted into the centre of the cakes comes out clean and the tops are golden.

5 Leave the cakes to cool in the tins for 5 minutes, then remove from the tins and leave to cool completely on wire racks.

VARIATION
Replace the lemon curd and fromage frais filling with a lemon syrup. Boil 45ml/3 tbsp lemon juice, 15ml/1 tbsp lemon rind and 30ml/2 tbsp caster sugar for 3 minutes until syrupy and glossy. Make a single cake using half the ingredients. Pour the syrup over the warm cake and leave to cool.

6 To finish, spread one cake with the lemon curd and spoon the fromage frais evenly over the lemon curd. Put the second cake on top, press down gently, then dust the top with icing sugar before serving.

SUMMER

Cooking hot meals in the height of summer is no-one's idea of fun, although presiding over a glowing barbecue is a popular pastime. Appetites are slighter at this time of year, so the keynote of summer cooking is simple, but tasty meals. Whether making chilled soups, salads, pasta or grilled food, the easiest way to achieve success is to take advantage of the mass of fresh herbs that flourish in the summer months.

There is no simpler or quicker way to turn a pan-fried main course – whether meat or fish – into something special, than to serve it topped with a herb butter. Freshly made herb salsa requires hardly any more effort and there are numerous other ways to enjoy this characteristic flavour of summer. Sprinkle fresh herbs on the hot coals of a barbe-

cue to create a wonderful aroma while you are cooking, and don't forget that you can use stripped rosemary stems instead of skewers for savoury kebabs or treat your guests to fruity Lemon Grass Skewers with Bay Leaves for a fabulous barbecue dessert. Give tarts and pizzas a lavish topping of fresh herbs or let their flavours mingle in oven-baked parcels that can be left to cook to perfection while you sip a glass of chilled wine in the shade.

Some combinations of herbs and vegetables seem to have been made for each other. Basil and tomatoes, whether raw in a simple salad or cooked as in Tomato and Fresh Basil Soup, almost define summer eating. In fact, basil goes well with almost all the seasonal vegetables, from peas to (bell) peppers. Garlic and almonds is a popular Mediterranean partnership, while chives with chillies and ginger, or with lime and lemon grass evoke the flavours of Asia. This chapter also includes some more unusual and adventurous flavourings. Lavender, for example, might not spring to mind immediately as a culinary herb, yet its intense fragrance makes it a perfect partner to lamb. You might also like to try Lavender and Honey Ice Cream for a sensational dessert or use the flowers to make a charming garnish.

CHILLED GARLIC <u>AND</u> ALMOND SOUP <u>WITH</u> GRAPES

USE PLUMP GARLIC CLOVES FOR THIS RICHLY FLAVOURED AND CREAMY CHILLED SOUP, WHICH IS BASED ON AN ANCIENT MOORISH RECIPE FROM ANDALUCIA IN SOUTHERN SPAIN. ALMONDS AND PINE NUTS COMPLETE THE FULL FLAVOUR.

3 Soak the bread in 300ml/½ pint/ 1¼ cups of the water for 10 minutes, then squeeze dry. Process the garlic, bread, nuts and 5ml/1 tsp salt to a paste in a food processor or blender.

4 Gradually blend in the olive oil and sherry vinegar, followed by sufficient water to make a smooth soup with a creamy consistency.

5 Stir in 30ml/2 tbsp of the sherry. Adjust the seasoning and add more dry sherry to taste. Chill for at least 3 hours, then adjust the seasoning again and stir in a little more iced water if the soup has thickened. Reserve a few of the grapes for the garnish and stir the remainder into the soup.

6 Ladle the soup into bowls (glass bowls look good) and garnish with ice cubes, the reserved grapes and chopped chives. Serve with additional extra virgin olive oil for drizzling to taste over the soup just before it is eaten.

<u>SERVES SIX</u>

INGREDIENTS
   75g/3oz/½ cup blanched almonds
   50g/2oz/½ cup pine nuts
   6 large garlic cloves, peeled but
     left whole
   200g/7oz good-quality day-old bread,
     crusts removed
   900ml–1 litre/1½–1¾ pints/3¾–
     4 cups still mineral water, chilled
   120ml/4fl oz/½ cup extra virgin olive
     oil, plus extra to serve
   15ml/1 tbsp sherry vinegar
   30–45ml/2–3 tbsp dry sherry
   250g/9oz grapes, peeled, halved
     and seeded
   salt and ground white pepper
   ice cubes and chopped fresh chives,
     to garnish

1 Roast the almonds and pine nuts together in a dry pan over a moderate heat until they are very lightly browned. Allow to cool, then grind to a powder.

2 Blanch the peeled garlic cloves in boiling water for 3 minutes, then drain and rinse.

COOK'S TIPS
• Blanching the garlic softens its flavour.
• Toasting the nuts slightly accentuates their flavour, but you can omit this step if you prefer a paler soup.

TOMATO AND FRESH BASIL SOUP

FRESH BASIL AND FULL-FLAVOURED TOMATOES ARE A FAVOURITE COMBINATION. MAKE THIS DELICIOUS ITALIAN SOUP IN LATE SUMMER WHEN TOMATOES ARE AT THEIR BEST AND THERE IS STILL PLENTY OF FRESH BASIL TO BE PICKED.

SERVES FOUR

INGREDIENTS

15ml/1 tbsp olive oil
1 onion, finely chopped
900g/2lb plum tomatoes, chopped
1 garlic clove, roughly chopped
about 750ml/1¼ pints/3 cups
    chicken or vegetable stock
120ml/4fl oz/½ cup dry white wine
30ml/2 tbsp sun-dried tomato purée
    (paste)
30ml/2 tbsp chopped fresh basil,
    plus a few whole leaves to garnish
30ml/2 tbsp single (light) cream
salt and ground black pepper

1 Heat the olive oil in a large pan over a medium heat. Add the chopped onion and cook it gently for about 5 minutes, stirring frequently, until it is softened but not brown.

2 Stir in the chopped tomatoes and garlic, then add the stock, white wine and tomato purée, with seasoning to taste. Bring to the boil, then reduce the heat, half-cover the pan and simmer for 20 minutes, stirring occasionally.

3 Purée the soup with the chopped basil in a food processor or blender, then press through a sieve into a clean pan. Discard the residue in the sieve.

4 Add the cream to the pan and heat through, stirring. Do not allow the soup to boil. Check the consistency and add more hot stock if necessary, then add the seasoning. Pour into bowls and garnish with basil leaves. Serve at once.

ITALIAN PEA AND BASIL SOUP

THE PUNGENT FLAVOUR OF BASIL LIFTS THIS APPETIZING ITALIAN SOUP OF PETITS POIS, WHILE THE ONION AND GARLIC GIVE DEPTH. SERVE IT WITH GOOD CRUSTY BREAD TO ENJOY IT AT ITS BEST.

2 Add the peas and stock to the pan and bring to the boil. Reduce the heat, add the basil and seasoning, then simmer for 10 minutes.

3 Spoon the soup into a food processor or blender (you may have to do this in batches) and process until the soup is smooth.

4 Return the soup to the rinsed pan and reheat gently until piping hot. Ladle into warm bowls, sprinkle with shaved Parmesan and garnish with basil.

SERVES FOUR

INGREDIENTS
   75ml/5 tbsp olive oil
   2 large onions, chopped
   1 celery stick, chopped
   1 carrot, chopped
   1 garlic clove, finely chopped
   400g/14oz/3½ cups frozen
     petits pois (baby peas)
   900ml/1½ pints/3¾ cups
     vegetable stock
   25g/1oz/1 cup fresh basil leaves,
     roughly torn, plus extra to garnish
   salt and ground black pepper
   shaved Parmesan cheese,
     to serve

1 Heat the oil in a large pan and add the onions, celery, carrot and garlic. Cover the pan and cook over a low heat for 45 minutes, or until the vegetables are soft, stirring occasionally to prevent the vegetables sticking.

VARIATION
You can also use mint or a mixture of parsley, mint and chives in place of the basil, if you like.

BAKED VEGETABLES <u>WITH</u> THYME

CRUNCHY GOLDEN BATTER SURROUNDS THIS ATTRACTIVE COMBINATION OF BRIGHT PEPPERS, ONION, AUBERGINE AND COURGETTES. FLAVOURED WITH THYME, THEY ARE BOTH DELICIOUS AND FILLING, AND, SERVED WITH SALAD, MAKE AN EXCELLENT LIGHT LUNCH.

SERVES SIX

INGREDIENTS
   1 small aubergine (eggplant),
      trimmed, halved and thickly sliced
   1 egg
   115g/4oz/1 cup plain (all-purpose)
      flour
   300ml/½ pint/1¼ cups milk
   30ml/2 tbsp fresh thyme leaves,
      or 10ml/2 tsp dried
   1 red onion
   2 large courgettes (zucchini)
   1 red (bell) pepper
   1 yellow (bell) pepper
   60–75ml/4–5 tbsp sunflower oil
   30ml/2 tbsp freshly grated
      (shredded) Parmesan cheese
   salt and ground black pepper
   fresh herbs, to garnish

1 Place the aubergine in a colander or sieve, sprinkle generously with salt, and leave for 10 minutes. Drain, rinse well and pat dry on kitchen paper.

2 Meanwhile, beat the egg in a bowl, then gradually beat in the flour and a little milk to make a smooth, thick paste. Gradually blend in the rest of the milk, add the thyme and seasoning to taste, and stir until smooth. Leave in a cool place until required. Preheat the oven to 220°C/425°F/Gas 7.

COOK'S TIP
It is essential to get the fat in the roasting pan really hot before adding the batter, which should sizzle slightly as it goes in. Use a pan that is not too deep.

3 Quarter the onion, slice the courgettes and seed and quarter the peppers. Put the oil in a roasting pan and heat in the oven. Add the vegetables, including the aubergines, toss in the oil to coat thoroughly and return to the oven for 20 minutes.

4 Whisk the batter, then pour it over the vegetables and return to the oven for 30 minutes. When puffed up and golden, reduce the heat to 190°C/375°F/Gas 5 for 10–15 minutes, or until crisp around the edges. Sprinkle with Parmesan and herbs, and serve.

ROASTED PEPPERS <u>WITH</u> SWEET CICELY

The sweet aniseed flavours of sweet cicely and fennel combine beautifully with the succulent tastes of the peppers and tomatoes and the piquancy of capers. Sweet cicely leaves make an excellent garnish and they taste just like the flowers. This dish can be served as a light lunch or as an unusual starter for a dinner party.

3 Place a whole small or half a medium tomato in each half of a pepper cavity.

4 Cover with a scattering of semi-ripe sweet cicely seeds, fennel seeds and capers and about half the sweet cicely flowers. Drizzle the olive oil all over.

5 Bake in the top of the oven for 1 hour. Remove from the oven and add the rest of the flowers. Garnish with fresh sweet cicely leaves and flowers, and serve with lots of crusty bread to soak up the juices.

SERVES FOUR

INGREDIENTS
    4 red (bell) peppers, halved
      and deseeded
    8 small or 4 medium tomatoes
    15ml/1 tbsp semi-ripe sweet
      cicely seeds
    15ml/1 tbsp fennel seeds
    15ml/1 tbsp capers
    8 sweet cicely flowers, newly
      opened, stems removed
    60ml/4 tbsp olive oil
For the garnish
    a few small sweet cicely leaves
    8 more flowers

1 Preheat the oven to 180°C/350°F/ Gas 4. Place the red pepper halves in a large ovenproof dish and set aside.

2 To skin the tomatoes, cut a cross at the base, then pour over boiling water and leave them to stand for 30 seconds to 1 minute. Cut them in half if they are of medium size.

COOK'S TIP
Try adding the stems from the sweet cicely to the water in which fruit is stewed. They will add a delightful flavour and reduce the need for sugar.

VARIATION
If sweet cicely is not available, this dish can also be made with a range of different herbs, although they will all impart a distinctive flavour. Celery leaves, chervil and lovage are some you might like to try.

SALMON EN PAPILLOTE <u>WITH</u> CHILLIES <u>AND</u> CHIVES

COOKING FISH "EN PAPILLOTE" ENSURES THAT THE AROMATIC INGREDIENTS RETAIN THEIR FLAVOUR, AND THAT THE SALMON REMAINS MOIST AND SUCCULENT. IT IS ALSO EXCELLENT WHEN ENTERTAINING, AS THE PARCELS MAY BE PREPARED AHEAD OF COOKING.

SERVES SIX

INGREDIENTS
    25ml/1½ tbsp groundnut (peanut) oil
    2 yellow (bell) peppers, seeded and
        thinly sliced
    4cm/1½in fresh root ginger, peeled
        and finely grated (shredded)
    1 large fennel bulb, finely sliced,
        feathery tops chopped and reserved
    1 fresh green chilli, seeded and
        finely sliced
    2 large leeks, cut into 10cm/4in
        lengths and sliced lengthways
    60ml/4 tbsp chopped chives
    10ml/2 tsp light soy sauce
    6 portions salmon fillet, about
        175g/6oz each, skinned
    10ml/2 tsp toasted sesame oil
    salt and ground black pepper

1 Heat the oil in a large, non-stick frying pan and cook the peppers, ginger and fennel for 5–6 minutes, or until they are softened but not browned. Add the chilli and leeks and cook for a further 2–3 minutes. Stir in half the chives and the soy sauce with seasoning to taste. Set aside to cool.

2 Preheat the oven to 190°C/375°F/ Gas 5. Cut six 35cm/14in circles of baking parchment or foil. Divide the vegetable mixture among the circles and place a portion of salmon on top. Drizzle with sesame oil and sprinkle with the remaining chives and the chopped fennel tops. Season to taste.

3 Fold the paper or foil over to enclose the fish, rolling and twisting the edges together to seal the parcels.

4 Place the parcels on a baking tray and bake for 15–20 minutes, or until the parcels are puffed up and, if made with paper, lightly browned. Transfer the parcels to warmed individual plates and serve immediately.

COOK'S TIP
This dish is excellent served with a simple accompaniment such as buttered new potatoes or plain egg noodles.

GRILLED SOLE WITH CHIVE, LIME AND LEMON GRASS BUTTER

CHIVES MIXED WITH PIQUANT LIME AND LEMON GRASS MAKE A DELICIOUS BUTTER TO SERVE WITH SIMPLE GRILLED FISH. SOLE IS THE IDEAL CHOICE, BUT HALIBUT AND TURBOT ARE ALSO GOOD. SERVE WITH STEAMED NEW POTATOES AND A SIMPLE VEGETABLE ACCOMPANIMENT.

SERVES FOUR

INGREDIENTS

115g/4oz/½ cup unsalted (sweet) butter, plus extra melted butter
5ml/1 tsp minced (ground) or very finely chopped lemon grass
pinch of finely grated lime rind
1 kaffir lime leaf, very finely sliced (optional)
45ml/3 tbsp finely chopped chives or chive flowers
2.5–5ml/½–1 tsp Thai fish sauce (*nam pla*)
4 sole, skinned
salt and ground black pepper
a few whole chives and/or chive flowers, to garnish
lemon or lime wedges, to serve

1 Cream the butter with the lemon grass, lime rind, kaffir lime leaf, if using, and chives or chive flowers. Season to taste with Thai fish sauce (*nam pla*), salt and pepper.

2 Chill the butter to firm it briefly, then form it into a roll and wrap in foil or clear film (plastic wrap). Chill until firm.

3 Heat the grill (broiler). Brush the sole with a little melted butter and season to taste. Grill (broil) for about 5 minutes on each side, or until firm and just cooked.

4 Slice the butter. Place the fish on warmed plates and top with butter. Decorate with chives and hand round lemon or lime wedges.

SARDINES <u>WITH</u> WARM HERB SALSA

PLAIN GRILLING OR BARBECUING IS THE VERY BEST WAY TO COOK FRESH SARDINES. SERVED WITH THIS LUSCIOUS SALSA OF PARSLEY, CHIVES AND BASIL, THE ONLY OTHER ESSENTIAL INGREDIENT IS FRESH, CRUSTY BREAD, TO MOP UP THE TASTY JUICES.

SERVES FOUR

INGREDIENTS
   12–16 fresh sardines
   oil for brushing
   juice of 1 lemon
   crusty bread, to serve
For the salsa
   15ml/1 tbsp butter
   4 spring onions (scallions), chopped
   1 garlic clove, finely chopped
   rind of 1 lemon
   30ml/2 tbsp finely chopped
     fresh parsley
   30ml/2 tbsp finely chopped
     fresh chives
   30ml/2 tbsp finely chopped
     fresh basil
   30ml/2 tbsp green olive paste
   10ml/2 tsp balsamic vinegar
   salt and ground black pepper

3 Add the lemon rind and remaining salsa ingredients to the onions and garlic in the pan and keep warm, stirring occasionally. Do not allow the mixture to boil.

4 Brush the sardines lightly with oil and sprinkle with lemon juice and seasoning. Cook for about 2 minutes on each side, on a barbecue or under a moderate grill (broiler). Serve with the salsa and bread.

1 To clean the sardines, use a pair of small kitchen scissors to slit the fish along the belly and pull out the innards. Wipe the fish with kitchen paper, and then arrange on a grill rack (broiler).

2 To make the salsa, melt the butter in a small pan and gently sauté the spring onions and garlic for about 2 minutes, shaking the pan occasionally, until softened but not browned.

COOK'S TIP
It is important to remove the innards as soon as possible, or they will start to taint the surrounding flesh.

VEAL CHOPS <u>WITH</u> BASIL BUTTER

VEAL CHOPS FROM THE LOIN ARE AN EXPENSIVE CUT AND ARE BEST COOKED QUICKLY AND SIMPLY. THE FLAVOURS OF BASIL AND DIJON MUSTARD GO WELL WITH VEAL AND ARE SUPERB IN A MELTING BUTTER. NEW POTATOES AND A MIXED SALAD ARE PERFECT ACCOMPANIMENTS.

<u>SERVES TWO</u>

INGREDIENTS
    2 veal loin chops, 2.5cm/1in thick,
      about 225g/8oz each
    olive oil, for brushing
    salt and ground black pepper
    fresh basil sprigs, to garnish
For the basil butter
    25g/1oz/2 tbsp butter, softened
    15ml/1 tbsp Dijon mustard
    15ml/1 tbsp chopped fresh basil

1 To make the basil butter, cream the softened butter with the Dijon mustard and chopped fresh basil in a large mixing bowl, then season with plenty of freshly ground black pepper.

2 Brush both sides of each chop with olive oil and season with a little salt.

3 Cook the chops on a hot griddle or in a heavy frying pan for 7–10 minutes, basting with oil and turning once, until done to your liking. (Medium-rare meat will still be slightly soft when pressed, medium meat will be springy, and well-done firm.) Top each chop with half the basil butter and serve at once, garnished with basil.

LAMB <u>WITH</u> LAVENDER BALSAMIC MARINADE

FRAGRANT LAVENDER IS AN UNUSUAL FLAVOUR TO USE WITH MEAT, BUT ITS HEADY, SUMMERY SCENT WORKS WELL WITH GRILLED OR BARBECUED LAMB. IF YOU PREFER, ROSEMARY CAN TAKE ITS PLACE.

SERVES FOUR

INGREDIENTS
  4 racks of lamb, with 3–4 cutlets
    on each
  1 shallot, finely chopped
  45ml/3 tbsp chopped fresh lavender
    florets, plus extra to garnish
  15ml/1 tbsp balsamic vinegar
  30ml/2 tbsp olive oil
  15ml/1 tbsp lemon juice
  salt and ground black pepper
  handful of lavender sprigs

1 Place the racks of lamb in a large mixing bowl or wide dish and sprinkle over the chopped shallot.

2 Sprinkle the chopped fresh lavender over the racks of lamb.

3 Beat together the balsamic vinegar, olive oil and lemon juice and pour them over the lamb. Season well with salt and ground black pepper and then turn the meat to coat it evenly.

4 Scatter a few of the lavender sprigs over the grill (broiler) or on the coals of a medium-hot barbecue. Cook the lamb for about 15–20 minutes, turning once and basting with any remaining marinade.

5 Serve the lamb while it is still slightly pink in the centre, garnished with the remaining lavender.

CHICKEN AND CORIANDER SALAD

SERVE THIS SUBSTANTIAL SUMMER SALAD WARM TO MAKE THE MOST OF THE WONDERFUL FLAVOURS OF CHICKEN AND CORIANDER. THE CHICKEN CAN BE GRILLED OR IS ALSO EXCELLENT BARBECUED.

2 Cook the mangetouts for 2 minutes in boiling water, then refresh in cold water. Tear the lettuces into small pieces and mix all the salad ingredients and the bacon together. Arrange the salad in individual dishes.

3 Season the chicken breasts with salt and pepper, then grill (broil) them on medium heat for 10–15 minutes, or cook on a medium barbecue. Baste with the marinade and turn once during cooking, until cooked through.

SERVES SIX

INGREDIENTS
   4 medium chicken breasts, skinned
     and boned
   225g/8oz mangetouts (snow peas)
   2 heads decorative lettuce such as
     lollo rosso or feuille de chêne
   3 carrots, cut into matchsticks
   175g/6oz/2⅓ cups sliced
     button (white) mushrooms
   6 bacon rashers (strips), fried
     and chopped
   salt and ground black pepper
   60ml/4 tbsp fresh coriander
     (cilantro) leaves
For the coriander dressing
   120ml/4fl oz/½ cup lemon juice
   30ml/2 tbsp wholegrain mustard
   250ml/8fl oz/1 cup olive oil
   75ml/2½fl oz/⅓ cup sesame oil
   5ml/1 tsp coriander seeds, crushed

1 Mix all the dressing ingredients in a bowl. Place the prepared chicken breasts in a shallow dish and pour over half the dressing. Leave to marinate overnight in the refrigerator. Chill the remaining dressing.

COOK'S TIP
Use any of your favourite herbs in this dish, basil, parsley and thyme all work well.

4 Slice the chicken into thin pieces. Divide among the bowls of salad and add some of the dressing to each dish. Combine quickly and scatter some fresh coriander over each bowl, to garnish.

ONION TART

*THIS CLASSIC ONION TART, FLAVOURED WITH NUTMEG, COMES FROM ALSACE IN EASTERN FRANCE.
IT IS TRADITIONALLY SERVED IN SMALL SLICES AS A FIRST COURSE, BUT IT ALSO MAKES A DELICIOUS
WARM MAIN COURSE WHEN ACCOMPANIED BY A GREEN SALAD.*

SERVES FOUR TO SIX

INGREDIENTS
   175g/6oz/1½ cups plain
      (all-purpose) flour
   75g/3oz/6 tbsp butter, chilled
   30–45ml/2–3 tbsp iced water
For the filling
   50g/2oz/¼ cup butter
   900g/2lb Spanish onions,
      sliced
   1 egg plus 2 egg yolks
   250ml/8fl oz/1 cup double
      (heavy) cream
   1.5ml/¼ tsp freshly grated
      (shredded) nutmeg
   salt and ground black pepper

1 Process the flour, a pinch of salt and the butter in a food processor until reduced to fine crumbs. Or, rub the fat into the flour using the fingertips. Add the iced water and process, or knead, briefly to form a dough. Gather into a ball and chill for 40 minutes.

2 Meanwhile, start the filling. Melt the butter in a large pan and add the onions and a pinch of salt. Turn them in the butter. Cover and cook very gently, stirring frequently, for 30–40 minutes. The onions should gradually turn golden yellow. Cool slightly.

VARIATIONS
There are endless variations on this classic tart: try adding chopped fresh herbs, such as thyme, or, for meat-eaters, 115g/4oz/⅔ cup chopped smoked pancetta.

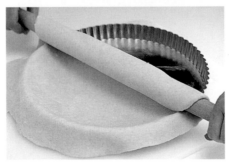

3 Preheat the oven to 190°C/375°F/Gas 5. Roll out the dough thinly and use to line a 23–25cm/9–10in loose-based flan tin (quiche pan). Line with baking parchment and baking beans, then bake blind for 10 minutes.

4 Remove the paper and baking beans and bake for 4–5 minutes more, until the pastry is lightly cooked to a pale brown (blonde is quite a good description). Reduce the oven setting to 180°C/350°F/Gas 4.

5 Beat the egg, egg yolks and cream together. Season with salt, lots of black pepper and the grated nutmeg. Place half the onions in the pastry shell and add half the egg mixture. Add the remaining onions, then pour in as much of the remaining custard as you can.

6 Place on a baking sheet and bake on the middle shelf for 40–50 minutes, or until the custard is risen, browned and set in the centre. Serve warm rather than piping hot.

PENNE <u>WITH</u> ROCKET <u>AND</u> MOZZARELLA

LIKE A WARM SALAD, THIS PASTA DISH IS VERY QUICK AND EASY TO MAKE — PERFECT FOR AN AL FRESCO SUMMER LUNCH. CRISP ROCKET AND GOOD-QUALITY, FRESH AND RIPE TOMATOES PROVIDE THE ESSENTIAL FLAVOURINGS HERE.

SERVES FOUR

INGREDIENTS
  400g/14oz/3½ cups fresh or
    dried penne
  6 ripe plum tomatoes, peeled, seeded
    and diced
  2 × 150g/5oz packets mozzarella
    cheese, drained and diced
  2 large handfuls of rocket (arugula),
    total weight about 150g/5oz
  75ml/5 tbsp extra virgin olive oil
  salt and ground black pepper

VARIATION
For a change, a mixture of basil and
rocket leaves also works well.

1 Cook the fresh or dried pasta in a
large pan of boiling salted water
according to the packet instructions
until it is *al dente*.

2 Meanwhile, put the diced tomatoes,
mozzarella, rocket and olive oil into a
large bowl with a little salt and ground
black pepper to taste and toss
everything together well to mix.

3 Drain the cooked pasta and tip it into
the bowl with the other ingredients. Toss
well to mix and serve immediately.

COOK'S TIP
To keep the pasta shapes separate, stir
it frequently during cooking. This is
especially important at the start of the
cooking process.

FUSILLI <u>WITH</u> BASIL <u>AND</u> PEPPERS

CHARGRILLED PEPPERS HAVE A WONDERFUL, SMOKY FLAVOUR THAT MARRIES WELL WITH GARLIC, OLIVES, BASIL AND TOMATOES IN THIS DELECTABLE PASTA DISH.

SERVES FOUR

INGREDIENTS
  3 large (bell) peppers (red, yellow
    and orange)
  350g/12oz/3 cups fresh or
    dried fusilli
  60ml/4 tbsp extra virgin olive oil
  1–2 garlic cloves, to taste,
    finely chopped
  4 ripe plum tomatoes, peeled, seeded
    and diced
  50g/2oz/½ cup pitted black olives,
    halved or quartered lengthways
  1 handful of fresh basil leaves
  salt and ground black pepper

VARIATION
Add a few slivers of bottled or canned
anchovy fillets at step 5.

1 Put the whole peppers under a hot
grill (broiler) and grill (broil) for about
10 minutes, turning frequently until
charred on all sides.

2 Put the hot peppers in a plastic bag,
seal the bag and set aside until the
peppers are cold.

3 Remove the peppers from the bag
and hold them, one at a time, under
cold running water. Peel off the charred
skins with your fingers, split the
peppers open and pull out the cores.
Rub off all the seeds under the running
water, then pat the peppers dry on
kitchen paper.

4 Cook the pasta in salted boiling water
until *al dente*.

5 Meanwhile, thinly slice the peppers
and place them in a large bowl with the
olive oil, garlic, tomatoes, olives, basil,
salt and pepper to taste.

6 Drain the cooked pasta and tip it into
the bowl with the other ingredients. Toss
well to mix and serve immediately.

New Potato, Rosemary and Garlic Pizza

Waxy new potatoes, smoked mozzarella, rosemary and garlic make the flavour of this pizza unique. For a delicious variation, use sage instead of rosemary.

SERVES TWO TO THREE

INGREDIENTS
  350g/12oz new potatoes
  45ml/3 tbsp olive oil
  2 garlic cloves, crushed
  1 pizza base, 25–30cm/10–12in
    diameter
  1 red onion, thinly sliced
  150g/5oz/1¼ cups grated (shredded)
    smoked mozzarella cheese
  10ml/2 tsp chopped fresh rosemary
  salt and ground black pepper
  30ml/2 tbsp freshly grated Parmesan,
    to garnish

1 Preheat the oven to 220°C/425°F/ Gas 7. Scrape the potatoes and cook in boiling salted water for 5 minutes. Drain well. When cool, peel and slice thinly.

2 Heat 30ml/2 tbsp of the oil in a frying pan. Add the sliced potatoes and garlic and fry for 5–8 minutes, or until tender.

3 Brush the pizza base with the remaining oil. Scatter over the onion, then arrange the potatoes on top.

4 Sprinkle over the mozzarella and rosemary. Grind over plenty of black pepper and bake for 15–20 minutes, or until crisp and golden. Remove from the oven and sprinkle over the Parmesan to serve.

FETA, ROASTED GARLIC AND OREGANO PIZZA

THIS IS A PIZZA FOR GARLIC LOVERS! MASH DOWN THE CLOVES AS YOU EAT — THEY SHOULD BE SOFT AND WILL HAVE LOST THEIR PUNGENCY. FRESH OREGANO PROVIDES THE FINISHING TOUCH.

5 Place the peppers skin-side up on a baking sheet and grill (broil) evenly. Put in a covered bowl for 10 minutes. Peel off the skins. Cut the flesh into strips.

6 Put the tomatoes in a bowl and pour over boiling water. Leave for 30 seconds, then plunge into cold water. Peel, seed and roughly chop the flesh.

7 Divide the dough into four. Roll out each on flour to a 14cm/5½in circle.

8 Place on greased baking sheets, then push up the dough edges. Brush with half the oil and add the tomatoes, peppers, feta and garlic. Drizzle over the remaining oil and season. Bake for 15–20 minutes. Garnish with oregano.

SERVES FOUR

INGREDIENTS
1 medium garlic bulb, unpeeled
45ml/3 tbsp olive oil
1 medium red bell pepper, quartered and seeded
1 medium yellow bell pepper, quartered and seeded
2 plum tomatoes
175g/6oz feta cheese, crumbled
ground black pepper
15–30ml/1–2 tbsp chopped fresh oregano, to garnish

For the pizza dough
175g/6oz/1½ cups strong white bread flour, plus extra for dusting
1.5ml/¼ tsp salt
5ml/1 tsp easy-blend (rapid-rise) dried yeast
120–150ml/4–5fl oz/½–⅔ cup lukewarm water
15ml/1 tbsp olive oil

1 To make the dough, sift the flour and salt into a bowl. Stir in the yeast. Make a well in the centre of the ingredients. Pour in the water and oil and mix to a soft dough.

2 Knead the dough on a lightly floured surface for about 10 minutes until smooth and elastic, then place in a greased bowl and cover with clear film. Leave in a warm place to rise for about 1 hour, or until doubled in size.

3 Knock back (punch down) the dough, and knead again for 2–3 minutes.

4 Preheat the oven to 220°C/425°F/ Gas 7. Break the garlic into cloves, discarding the outer papery leaves. Toss in 15ml/1 tbsp of the oil.

GREEK YOGURT AND FIG CAKE

BAKED FRESH FIGS, THICKLY SLICED, MAKE A DELECTABLE TOPPING FOR A FEATHERLIGHT SPONGE.
FIGS THAT ARE A BIT ON THE FIRM SIDE WORK BEST FOR THIS PARTICULAR RECIPE.

SERVES SIX TO EIGHT

INGREDIENTS
  6 firm fresh figs, thickly sliced
  45ml/3 tbsp clear honey, plus extra
    for glazing
  200g/7oz/scant 1 cup butter,
    softened, plus extra for greasing
  175g/6oz/scant 1 cup caster
    (superfine) sugar
  grated (shredded) rind of 1 lemon
  grated (shredded) rind of 1 orange
  4 eggs, separated
  225g/8oz/2 cups plain (all-purpose)
    flour
  5ml/1 tsp baking powder
  5ml/1 tsp bicarbonate of soda
    (baking soda)
  250ml/8fl oz/1 cup Greek
    (US strained plain) yogurt

1 Preheat the oven to 180°C/350°F/
Gas 4. Grease a 23cm/9in cake tin
(pan) and line the base of it with
baking parchment.

2 Arrange the figs over the base of the
tin and drizzle over the honey.

3 In a large mixing bowl, cream the
butter and caster sugar with the lemon
and orange rinds until the mixture is
pale and fluffy, then gradually beat in
the egg yolks.

4 Sift the dry ingredients together in a
separate bowl. Add a little to the
creamed mixture, beat well, then beat
in a spoonful of Greek yogurt. Repeat
this process until all the dry ingredients
and Greek yogurt have been incorporated
into the creamed mixture.

5 Whisk the egg whites in a grease-free
bowl until they form stiff peaks. Stir half
the whites into the cake mixture to
slacken it slightly, then fold in the rest.
Pour the mixture over the figs in the
base of the cake tin.

6 Bake in the preheated oven for
1¼ hours, or until golden and a skewer
inserted in the centre of the cake
comes out clean.

7 Turn the cake out on to a wire rack,
peel off the lining paper and cool.
Drizzle the figs with a little extra honey
before serving.

LEMON GRASS SKEWERS WITH BAY LEAVES

GRILLED FRUITS MAKE A FINE FINALE TO A BARBECUE, WHETHER THEY ARE COOKED OVER THE COALS OR UNDER A HOT GRILL. THE LEMON GRASS SKEWERS GIVE THE FRUIT A SUBTLE LEMON TANG THAT IS COMPLEMENTED BY THE FLAVOUR OF THE BAY LEAVES. ALMOST ANY SOFT FRUITS CAN BE SUBSTITUTED.

SERVES FOUR

INGREDIENTS

4 long fresh lemon grass stalks
1 mango, peeled, stoned (pitted) and
    cut into chunks
1 papaya, peeled, seeded and cut
    into chunks
1 star fruit, cut into chunks
8 fresh bay leaves
oil, for greasing
a little nutmeg
60ml/4 tbsp maple syrup
50g/2oz/¼ cup demerara (raw) sugar
For the lime cheese
150g/5oz/⅔ cup curd (farmer's)
    cheese or low-fat soft cheese
120ml/4fl oz/½ cup double
    (heavy) cream
grated (shredded) rind and juice
    of ½ lime
30ml/2 tbsp icing (confectioners')
    sugar

1 Prepare the barbecue or preheat the grill (broiler). Cut the top of each lemon grass stalk into a point with a sharp knife. Discard the outer leaves, then use the back of the knife to bruise the length of each stalk to release the oils.

2 Thread each lemon grass stalk, skewer-style, with a selection of the fruit pieces and two bay leaves.

3 Support a piece of foil on a baking sheet and roll up the edges to make a rim. Grease the foil, lay the kebabs on top and grate a little nutmeg over each. Drizzle the maple syrup over and dust liberally with the demerara sugar. Grill (broil) or cook on a barbecue or 5 minutes, until the kebabs are lightly charred.

4 Meanwhile, make the lime cheese. Mix together the cheese, cream, grated lime rind and juice, and icing sugar in a bowl. Serve at once with the lightly charred fruit kebabs.

COOK'S TIP
Only fresh lemon grass will work as skewers. It is now possible to buy lemon grass stalks in jars.

GOOSEBERRY AND ELDERFLOWER FOOL

ELDERFLOWERS AND GOOSEBERRIES ARE A MATCH MADE IN HEAVEN, EACH BRINGING OUT THE FLAVOUR OF THE OTHER. SERVE WITH AMARETTI OR OTHER DESSERT BISCUITS FOR DIPPING.

SERVES SIX

INGREDIENTS

   450g/1lb/4 cups gooseberries,
     trimmed
   30ml/2 tbsp water
   50–75g/2–3oz/¼–⅓ cup caster
     (superfine) sugar
   30ml/2 tbsp elderflower cordial
   400g/14oz carton ready-made
     custard sauce
   300ml/½ pint/1¼ cups double
     (heavy) cream
   crushed amaretti, to decorate
   amaretti, to serve

1 Put the gooseberries and water in a pan. Cover and cook for 5–6 minutes.

2 Add the sugar and elderflower cordial to the gooseberries, then stir vigorously or mash until the fruit forms a pulp.

3 Remove the pan from the heat, spoon the gooseberry pulp into a bowl and set aside to cool.

4 Stir the custard into the fruit. Whip the cream to form soft peaks, then fold it into the mixture and chill.

5 Serve in dessert glasses, decorated with crushed amaretti, and accompanied by amaretti.

LAVENDER AND HONEY ICE CREAM

HONEY AND LAVENDER MAKE A MEMORABLE PARTNERSHIP IN THIS OLD-FASHIONED ICE CREAM. SERVE
SCOOPED INTO GLASSES OR SET IN LITTLE MOULDS AND TOP WITH LIGHTLY WHIPPED CREAM.

SERVES SIX TO EIGHT

INGREDIENTS
  90ml/6 tbsp clear honey
  4 egg yolks
  10ml/2 tsp cornflour (cornstarch)
  8 lavender spikes, plus extra,
   to decorate
  450ml/¾ pint/scant 2 cups milk
  450ml/¾ pint/scant 2 cups whipping
   cream
  dessert biscuits (cookies), to serve

1 Put the honey in a bowl together with
the egg yolks and cornflour. Pull the
lavender flowers from the spikes and
add them to the mixture in the bowl
with a little of the milk. Whisk lightly to
combine the ingredients.

2 Pour the remaining milk into a heavy
pan and bring it to the boil. Pour it over
the egg yolk mixture in the bowl, stirring
well with a wooden spoon as you pour.

3 Return the custard mixture to the pan
and cook it very gently, stirring constantly
with the wooden spoon until the mixture
thickens. Do not let it boil or it may curdle.

4 Pour the custard into a bowl, cover
the surface closely with greaseproof
(waxed) paper. Cool, then chill.

5 By hand: Whip the cream until it is
thickened but still falls from the whisk,
and stir into the custard. Transfer to a
freezerproof container. Freeze for about
6 hours, beating twice using a fork, a
whisk or a food processor to break up
the ice crystals. Freeze until firm.
Using an ice cream maker: Stir the
cream into the custard, then churn the
mixture in an ice cream maker until it
holds its shape. Transfer to a tub or
similar freezerproof container and
freeze until ready to serve.

6 Transfer the ice cream to the
refrigerator 30 minutes before serving,
so that it softens slightly. Scoop into
small dishes, decorate with lavender
flowers and serve with dessert biscuits.

CASHEW AND ORANGE FLOWER ICE CREAM

A CASHEW-NUT CREAM FORMS THE BASIS OF THIS DELICIOUS ICE CREAM, DELICATELY PERFUMED WITH ORANGE FLOWER WATER AND ORANGE RIND. IT EVOKES IMAGES OF ALL KINDS OF DESSERTS THAT ARE POPULAR IN THE MIDDLE EAST.

SERVES FOUR TO SIX

INGREDIENTS
4 egg yolks
75g/3oz/6 tbsp caster (superfine)
  sugar
5ml/1 tsp cornflour (cornstarch)
300ml/½ pint/1¼ cups semi-skimmed
  (low-fat) milk
150g/5oz/scant 1 cup cashew nuts
300ml/½ pint/1¼ cups whipping
  cream
15ml/1 tbsp orange flower water
grated (shredded) rind of ½ orange,
  plus curls of thinly pared orange
  rind, to decorate

1 Whisk the egg yolks, sugar and cornflour in a bowl until the mixture is thick and foamy. Pour the milk into a heavy pan, bring it to the boil, then gradually whisk it into the yolk mixture.

2 Return the mixture to the pan and cook over a gentle heat, stirring constantly until the custard thickens and is smooth. Do not let it boil or it may curdle. Pour it back into the bowl. Leave to cool, then chill.

COOK'S TIPS
• For a more intense flavour, roast the cashew nuts under the grill (broiler) or dry-fry before chopping them.
• To curl the thinly pared orange rind, wrap each strip in turn around a cocktail stick and leave it for a minute or two.

3 Very finely chop the cashew nuts. Heat the cream in a small pan. When it boils, stir in the nuts. Leave to cool.

4 Stir the orange flower water and grated orange rind into the chilled custard. Process the nut cream in a food processor or blender until it forms a fine paste, then stir it into the orange custard mixture.

5 By hand: Pour the mixture into a freezerproof container and freeze for 6 hours, beating twice with a fork, a whisk or an electric mixer to break up the ice crystals.
Using an ice cream maker: Churn the mixture until it is firm enough to scoop.

6 Scoop the ice cream into dishes and decorate with orange rind curls.

LEMON SORBET

THIS IS PROBABLY THE MOST CLASSIC SORBET OF ALL MADE WITH FRESH, JUICY LEMONS. REFRESHINGLY TANGY AND YET DELICIOUSLY SMOOTH, IT QUITE LITERALLY MELTS IN THE MOUTH.

SERVES SIX

INGREDIENTS
  200g/7oz/1 cup caster (superfine)
    sugar
  300ml/½ pint/1¼ cups water
  4 lemons, well scrubbed
  1 egg white
  sugared lemon rind, to decorate

1 Put the sugar and water into a pan and bring to the boil, stirring occasionally until the sugar dissolves.

2 Pare the rind thinly from two lemons so that it falls straight into the pan. Simmer for 2 minutes without stirring, then take the pan off the heat. Leave to cool, then chill.

3 Squeeze the juice from all the lemons and add it to the syrup.
By hand: Strain the syrup into a shallow freezerproof container, reserving the rind. Freeze the mixture for 4 hours until it is mushy.
Using an ice cream maker: Strain the syrup and lemon juice, and churn the mixture until thick.

4 By hand: Scoop the sorbet into a food processor and beat it until smooth. Lightly whisk the egg white with a fork until it is just frothy. Spoon the sorbet back into the tub, beat in the egg white and return the mixture to the freezer for 4 hours.
Using an ice cream maker: Add the egg white to the mixture and continue to churn for 10–15 minutes, or until firm enough to scoop.

5 Scoop into bowls or glasses and decorate with sugared lemon rind.

COOK'S TIP
Cut the top off a lemon and retain as a lid. Squeeze the juice out of the larger portion. Remove any membrane and use the shell as a container. Scoop sorbet into the shell, top with the lid and add lemon leaves or small bay leaves. Allow one lemon for each person.

VARIATION
Sorbet can be made from any citrus fruit. As a guide you will need 300ml/½ pint/ 1¼ cups fresh fruit juice and the pared rind of half the squeezed fruit. Use 4 oranges or 2 oranges and 2 lemons, or, for a grapefruit sorbet, use the rind of 1 ruby grapefruit and the juice of 2. For lime sorbet, combine the rind of 3 limes with the juice of 6.

AUTUMN

Autumn is the most glorious time of year from the culinary point of view. This is the season not just for the farmers' harvest of grains and orchard fruits, but also for wild mushrooms, nuts and young, tender root vegetables. All but the most summery of herbs are still abundant and the perennials, such as rosemary and bay, start to come into their own again now.

The nights are closing in and we begin to look for more warming and substantial supper dishes, but the short days are sometimes golden with sunshine, so lighter dishes, salads and even barbecue-cooked foods are not yet quite over. The recipes in this chapter offer a wide selection of dishes for the twin aspects of this sometimes capricious season. On chilly evenings or those days when winter

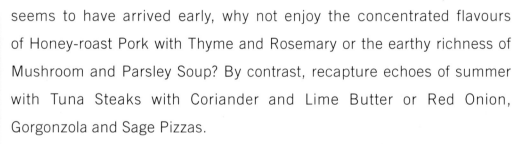

seems to have arrived early, why not enjoy the concentrated flavours of Honey-roast Pork with Thyme and Rosemary or the earthy richness of Mushroom and Parsley Soup? By contrast, recapture echoes of summer with Tuna Steaks with Coriander and Lime Butter or Red Onion, Gorgonzola and Sage Pizzas.

Autumn is a good season for the creative cook, when seasonal produce and year-round staples can be mixed and matched in delicious combinations. Those great convenience foods, pasta, cheese and eggs, are all enhanced by the addition of fresh herbs, while delicious salads harmonize superbly with a refreshing herb dressing.

Make a tour of your herb plot or check your window boxes to see which herbs are still flourishing and use them before the winter sets in. The recipe for Garlic and Herb Bread, for example, suggests using a mixture of parsley, chervil, tarragon and chives, but if it is too late in the year for chervil, you could substitute thyme, marjoram or even finely chopped rosemary.

MUSHROOM AND PARSLEY SOUP

A HANDFUL OF PARSLEY HARMONIZES WITH WHOLESOME FIELD MUSHROOMS, ENHANCING WITHOUT DOMINEERING THEIR FLAVOUR. THIS SOUP MAKES A HEARTY LUNCH, SERVED WITH CRUSTY BREAD, ON COLD AUTUMN DAYS.

SERVES EIGHT

INGREDIENTS
  75g/3oz/6 tbsp unsalted (sweet)
    butter
  2 onions, roughly chopped
  600ml/1 pint/2½ cups milk
  900g/2lb field (portabello)
    mushrooms, sliced
  8 slices white bread
  60ml/4 tbsp chopped fresh parsley,
    plus extra to garnish
  300ml/½ pint/1¼ cups double
    (heavy) cream
  salt and ground black pepper

COOK'S TIP
Use fresh flat leaf parsley in this soup. It
has a superior flavour to the curly variety.

1 Melt the butter and sauté the
chopped onion for about 5 minutes,
or until it is soft but not coloured. Add
the milk.

2 Add the sliced mushrooms to the
pan and continue cooking for a further
5 minutes.

3 Tear the bread into pieces, drop them
into the soup and leave to soak for
15 minutes. Purée the soup and return
it to the pan. Add the chopped parsley,
cream and salt and pepper to taste.
Reheat gently, but do not allow the soup
to boil. Serve at once, garnished with
extra chopped parsley.

SPICED ONION KOFTAS

CORIANDER, CUMIN, TURMERIC AND CHILLIES CREATE THE TRADITIONAL FLAVOURING FOR THESE INDIAN ONION FRITTERS. CHICKPEA FLOUR IS AVAILABLE FROM SUPERMARKETS AND INDIAN STORES.

SERVES FOUR TO FIVE

INGREDIENTS
   675g/1½lb onions, halved and
      thinly sliced
   5ml/1 tsp salt
   5ml/1 tsp ground coriander seeds
   5ml/1 tsp ground cumin
   2.5ml/½ tsp ground turmeric
   1–2 fresh green chillies, seeded and
      finely chopped
   45ml/3 tbsp chopped fresh
      coriander (cilantro)
   90g/3½oz/scant ¾ cup chickpea flour
   2.5ml/½ tsp baking powder
   vegetable oil, for deep-frying
To serve
   lemon wedges
   fresh coriander (cilantro) sprigs
   yogurt and herb dip or yogurt and
      cucumber dip (see Cook's Tips)

COOK'S TIPS
• To make a yogurt and herb dip, stir 30ml/2 tbsp each of chopped fresh coriander and mint into about 250ml/ 8fl oz/1 cup set yogurt. Season with salt, ground toasted cumin seeds and a pinch of muscovado (molasses) sugar.
• For a cucumber dip, stir half a diced cucumber and one seeded and chopped green chilli into 250ml/8fl oz/1 cup set yogurt. Season with salt and cumin.

1 Place the onions in a colander, add the salt and toss well. Stand the colander on a plate for 45 minutes, tossing once or twice. Rinse, then squeeze out excess moisture. Place in a bowl. Add the ground coriander, cumin, turmeric, chillies and fresh coriander. Mix well.

2 Add the chickpea flour and baking powder to the onion mixture, then use your hand to mix all the ingredients together thoroughly.

3 Shape the mixture by hand into 12–15 kofta, which should be about the size of golf balls.

4 Heat the oil for deep-frying to 180–190°C/350–375°F or until a cube of day-old bread browns in 30–45 seconds. Fry the kofta, four to five at a time, until deep golden brown all over.

5 Drain each batch on kitchen paper and keep warm until all the kofta are cooked. Serve with lemon wedges, coriander sprigs and a yogurt dip.

GRIDDLED FENNEL AND HERB SALAD WITH SPICY TOMATO DRESSING

THIS IS AN EXCELLENT SALAD TO MAKE IN THE EARLY AUTUMN WHEN DELICATELY SWEET FENNEL AND YOUNG LEEKS ARE AT THEIR BEST. THYME, BAY LEAVES, SHALLOTS, OLIVES AND A DASH OF CHILLI COMPLETE THE FUSION OF FLAVOURS. SERVE WITH GRILLED FISH OR SIMPLY WITH BREAD.

SERVES SIX AS A FIRST COURSE

INGREDIENTS
    675g/1½lb leeks
    2 large fennel bulbs
    120ml/4fl oz/½ cup extra virgin
      olive oil
    2 shallots, chopped
    150ml/¼ pint/⅔ cup dry white wine
      or white vermouth
    5ml/1 tsp fennel seeds, crushed
    6 fresh thyme sprigs
    2–3 bay leaves
    good pinch of dried red chilli flakes
    350g/12oz tomatoes, peeled, seeded
      and diced
    5ml/1 tsp sun-dried tomato
      paste (optional)
    good pinch of sugar (optional)
    75g/3oz/½ cup small black olives
    salt and ground black pepper

2 Trim the fennel bulbs with a sharp knife, reserving any feathery tops for the garnish and cut the bulbs either into thin slices or into thicker wedges, according to taste.

3 Cook the fennel in the reserved cooking water for about 5 minutes, then drain thoroughly and toss with 30ml/ 2 tbsp of the olive oil. Season to taste with black pepper.

6 Add the diced tomatoes and cook briskly for 5–8 minutes, or until reduced and thickened.

7 Add the tomato paste, if using, and adjust the seasoning, adding a good pinch of sugar, if you think the dressing needs it.

1 Cook the leeks in boiling salted water for 4–5 minutes. Use a draining spoon to remove the leeks, place them in a colander to drain thoroughly and cool. Reserve the cooking water in the pan. Then squeeze out excess water and cut the leeks into 7.5cm/3in lengths.

COOK'S TIP
When buying fennel, look for rounded bulbs; flatter ones are immature. The flesh should be crisp and white, with no signs of bruising. Avoid specimens with broken leaves or that appear to be either soggy or dried out.

4 Heat a ridged cast-iron griddle. Arrange the leeks and fennel slices or wedges on the griddle and cook until they are tinged deep brown. Remove the vegetables from the griddle, place in a large, shallow dish and set aside.

5 Place the remaining olive oil in a large pan with the shallots, white wine or vermouth, crushed fennel seeds, thyme, bay leaves and chilli flakes, and bring to the boil over a medium heat. Lower the heat and simmer for 10 minutes.

8 Pour the dressing over the leeks and fennel, toss to mix and leave to cool. The salad may be made several hours in advance and kept in the refrigerator, but bring it back to room temperature before serving.

9 When ready to serve, stir the salad and scatter the black olives and chopped fennel tops over the top.

VARIATION
If you prefer, the black olives can be served in a separate bowl, so that guests can help themselves if they wish.

Cod, Basil, Tomato and Potato Pie

Natural and smoked fish make a great combination, especially with a hint of tomato and basil. Served with a green salad, it makes an ideal dish for lunch or a family supper.

SERVES EIGHT

INGREDIENTS

1kg/2¼lb smoked cod
1kg/2¼lb white cod
900ml/1½ pints/3¾ cups milk
1.2 litres/2 pints/5 cups water
2 basil sprigs
1 lemon thyme sprig
150g/5oz/10 tbsp butter
1 onion, chopped
75g/3oz/⅔ cup plain (all-purpose)
   flour
30ml/2 tbsp chopped fresh basil
4 firm plum tomatoes, peeled
   and chopped
12 medium maincrop floury potatoes
salt and ground black pepper
crushed black peppercorns, to garnish
salad leaves, to serve

1 Place both kinds of fish in a roasting pan with 600ml/1 pint/2½ cups of the milk, the water and the herb sprigs. Bring to a simmer and cook gently for 3–4 minutes. Leave the fish to cool in the liquid for about 20 minutes. Drain the fish, reserving the cooking liquid for use in the sauce. Flake the fish, removing any skin and bone.

2 Melt 75g/3oz/6 tbsp of the butter in a large pan, add the onion and cook for about 5 minutes, or until softened and tender but not browned. Sprinkle over the flour and half the chopped basil. Gradually add the reserved fish cooking liquid, adding a little more milk if necessary to make a fairly thin sauce, and stirring constantly to make a smooth consistency. Bring to the boil, season with salt and pepper, and add the remaining basil.

3 Remove the pan from the heat, then add the fish and tomatoes and stir gently to combine. Pour into an ovenproof dish.

4 Preheat the oven to 180°C/350°F/ Gas 4. Cook the potatoes in boiling water until tender. Drain, then add the remaining butter and milk, and mash.

5 Season to taste and spoon over the fish mixture, using a fork to create a pattern. (You can freeze the pie at this stage.) Bake in the oven for 30 minutes, or until the top is golden. Sprinkle with the crushed peppercorns and serve hot with salad leaves.

TUNA STEAKS WITH CORIANDER AND LIME BUTTER

CORIANDER AND LIME COMPLEMENT EACH OTHER PERFECTLY IN THIS HERB BUTTER MELTED OVER TUNA STEAKS. A HERB BUTTER CAN TRANSFORM A SIMPLE MEAL AND CAN BE PREPARED IN ADVANCE, SO IT IS IDEAL FOR ENTERTAINING.

SERVES FOUR

INGREDIENTS

675g/1½lb tuna or swordfish, cut
   into 4 steaks, 2.5cm/1in thick
60ml/4 tbsp vegetable oil
30ml/2 tbsp tablespoons lemon juice
15ml/1 tbsp lime juice
salt and ground black pepper
slices of lime and parsley sprigs,
   to garnish
steamed asparagus, to serve (optional)
For the coriander and lime butter
25g/1oz/1 cup fresh coriander
   (cilantro)
225g/8oz/1 cup unsalted (sweet)
   butter, softened
grated (shredded) rind and juice of
   1 lime

1 To make the coriander and lime butter, finely chop the coriander leaves. Mix into the butter with the grated lime rind and juice. Transfer to greaseproof (waxed) paper and shape into a log. Chill.

2 Arrange the fish steaks in a dish. Combine the oil, citrus juices, salt and pepper and pour over the fish. Cover and chill for 1–2 hours, turning the fish once or twice. Preheat the grill (broiler).

VARIATIONS
• For Salmon Steaks with Citrus Butter, lightly brush four salmon steaks, 2.5cm/ 1in thick, with oil, and season. Grill for 4–5 minutes on each side. Serve topped with pats of citrus butter.

3 Drain the fish and arrange on the rack in the grill pan. Grill (broil) for 3–4 minutes, or until just firm to the touch but still moist in the centre, turning the steaks over once. Slice the butter.

4 Transfer the fish to warmed plates and top each fish steak with a pat of coriander-lime butter. Garnish with slices of lime and parsley sprigs and serve the fish immediately, accompanied by steamed asparagus, if you like.

SKEWERED LAMB WITH CORIANDER YOGURT

TENDER GRILLED OR BARBECUED LAMB IS MARINATED WITH THE AROMATIC FLAVOURS OF ONION, BAY, AND ROSEMARY, AND SERVED WITH A FRESH MINT AND CORIANDER YOGURT.

3 Mix together the onion, herbs, lemon rind and juice, sugar and oil, then season to taste.

4 Pour the marinade over the meat in the bowl and stir to ensure the meat is thoroughly covered. Cover with clear film and leave to marinate in the refrigerator for several hours.

SERVES FOUR

INGREDIENTS
    900g/2lb lean boneless lamb
    1 large onion, grated (shredded)
    3 bay leaves
    5 rosemary or thyme sprigs
    grated rind and juice of 1 lemon
    2.5ml/½ tsp caster (superfine) sugar
    75ml/2½fl oz/⅓ cup olive oil
    salt and ground black pepper
    sprigs of fresh rosemary, to garnish
    lemon wedges, to serve
For the coriander yogurt
    150ml/¼ pint/⅔ cup thick natural
      (plain) yogurt
    15ml/1 tbsp chopped fresh mint
    15ml/1 tbsp chopped fresh coriander
      (cilantro)
    10ml/2 tsp grated (shredded) onion

1 To make the coriander yogurt, mix together the natural yogurt, chopped fresh mint, chopped fresh coriander and grated onion. Transfer the mixture to a serving bowl.

2 To make the kebabs, cut the lamb into 2.5cm/1in cubes and put in a bowl.

5 Drain the meat and thread on to metal skewers. Cook under a hot grill (broiler), or on a barbecue, for about 10 minutes. Garnish with rosemary and serve with lemon wedges and the coriander yogurt (barbecue the lemon wedges as well, if you like).

COOK'S TIP
If possible, try to use real Greek (US strained plain) yogurt for the coriander yogurt in this recipe. Made from either sheep's or cow's milk, it is deliciously thick and creamy, and is also much less acidic than skimmed milk natural (plain) yogurt. American readers need to strain natural yogurt to thicken it up.

BEEF AND GRILLED SWEET POTATO SALAD WITH SHALLOT AND HERB DRESSING

THIS SALAD MAKES A GOOD MAIN DISH FOR A SUMMER BUFFET. IT HAS AN ABSOLUTELY DELICIOUS DRESSING OF MIXED HERBS AND DIJON MUSTARD, PERKED UP WITH A LITTLE GREEN CHILLI. SERVE WITH SOME PEPPERY SALAD LEAVES, SUCH AS WATERCRESS, MIZUNA OR ROCKET.

SERVES SIX TO EIGHT

INGREDIENTS
 800g/1¾lb fillet of beef
 5ml/1 tsp black peppercorns, crushed
 10ml/2 tsp chopped fresh thyme
 60ml/4 tbsp olive oil
 450g/1lb orange-fleshed sweet
  potato, peeled
 salt and ground black pepper
For the dressing
 1 garlic clove, chopped
 15g/½oz/½ cup flat leaf parsley
 30ml/2 tbsp chopped fresh
  coriander (cilantro)
 15ml/1 tbsp small salted
  capers, rinsed
 ½–1 fresh green chilli, seeded
  and chopped
 10ml/2 tsp Dijon mustard
 10–15ml/2–3 tsp white wine vinegar
 75ml/5 tbsp extra virgin olive oil
 2 shallots, finely chopped

1 Roll the beef in the peppercorns and thyme. Set aside to marinate. Heat the oven to 200°C/400°F/Gas 6.

2 Heat half the olive oil in a heavy frying pan. Add the marinated beef and brown it all over, turning frequently, to seal it. Place on a baking tray and cook in the preheated oven for 15–20 minutes.

3 Remove the beef from the oven, cover it with foil, then leave it to rest for 10–15 minutes.

4 Meanwhile, preheat the grill (broiler). Cut the sweet potatoes into 1cm/½in slices. Brush with the remaining oil, season to taste, and grill (broil) for 5–6 minutes on each side. Cut the sweet potato slices into strips and place them in a bowl.

5 Cut the beef into slices or strips and toss with the sweet potato, then set the bowl aside.

6 For the dressing, process the garlic, parsley, coriander, capers, chilli, mustard and 10ml/2 tsp of the vinegar in a food processor or blender until chopped. With the motor running, gradually pour in the oil to make a smooth dressing. Season the dressing with salt and pepper and add more vinegar, to taste. Stir in the shallots.

7 Toss the shallot and herb dressing into the sweet potatoes and beef and leave the salad to stand for up to 2 hours before serving.

HONEY-ROAST PORK WITH THYME AND ROSEMARY

LEAN PORK TENDERLOIN IS BAKED WITH A COVERING OF HONEY, MUSTARD, ROSEMARY AND THYME.
THE FLAVOURS ARE ROUNDED OFF WITH A GLORIOUS RED ONION CONFIT.

SERVES FOUR

INGREDIENTS
    450g/1lb pork tenderloin
    30ml/2 tbsp set (crystallized) honey
    30ml/2 tbsp Dijon mustard
    5ml/1 tsp chopped fresh rosemary
    2.5ml/½ tsp chopped fresh thyme
    1.5ml/¼ tsp whole tropical
        peppercorns
    sprigs of fresh rosemary and thyme,
        to garnish
    Anna potatoes (see Cook's Tip) and
        cauliflower, to serve
For the red onion confit
    4 red onions
    350ml/12fl oz/1½ cups
        vegetable stock
    15ml/1 tbsp red wine vinegar
    15ml/1 tbsp caster (superfine) sugar
    1 garlic clove, crushed
    30ml/2 tbsp ruby port
    pinch of salt

1 Preheat the oven to 180°C/350°F/
Gas 4. Trim off any visible fat from the
pork. Put the honey, mustard, rosemary
and thyme in a bowl and mix together.

2 Crush the peppercorns using a mortar
and pestle. Spread the honey mixture
over the pork and sprinkle with the
crushed peppercorns. Place in a non-
stick roasting pan and cook in the
preheated oven for 35–45 minutes.

3 To make the red onion confit; slice
the onions into rings and put them into
a heavy pan.

4 Add the stock, vinegar, sugar and
garlic to the pan. Bring to the boil, then
reduce the heat. Cover and simmer for
15 minutes.

5 Uncover and pour in the port and
continue to simmer the confit, stirring
occasionally, until the onions are soft
and the juices thick and syrupy. Season
to taste with salt.

6 Slice the pork. Serve garnished with
herbs and accompanied by the confit
and vegetables.

COOK'S TIP
For Anna potatoes, peel and thinly slice
potatoes. Arrange in layers in a dish.
Season each layer and dot with butter.
Cover with foil, and bake for 1 hour at
190°C/375°F/Gas 5.

ORECCHIETTE <u>WITH</u> ROCKET <u>AND</u> OREGANO

GARLIC AND TOMATOES ARE FREQUENT PARTNERS IN ITALIAN COOKING. IN THIS HEARTY DISH FROM PUGLIA IN SOUTH-EAST ITALY, ROCKET ADDS A PEPPERY DEFINITION TO A PASTA SAUCE.

SERVES FOUR TO SIX

INGREDIENTS
45ml/3 tbsp olive oil
1 small onion, finely chopped
300g/11oz canned chopped
   Italian plum tomatoes or passata
   (bottled strained tomatoes)
2.5ml/½ tsp dried oregano
pinch of chilli powder or
   cayenne pepper
30ml/2 tbsp red or white wine
2 potatoes, total weight about
   200g/7oz, diced
300g/11oz/2¾ cups dried orecchiette
2 garlic cloves, finely chopped
150g/5oz rocket (arugula) leaves,
   stalks removed
90g/3½oz/scant ½ cup ricotta cheese
salt and ground black pepper
freshly grated (shredded) Pecorino
   cheese, to serve

1 Heat 15ml/1 tbsp of the olive oil in a medium pan, add half the finely chopped onion and cook gently, stirring frequently, for about 5 minutes, or until softened. Add the canned tomatoes or passata, oregano and chilli powder or cayenne pepper to the onion. Pour the wine over, and add a little salt and pepper to taste. Cover the pan and simmer for about 15 minutes, stirring the mixture occasionally.

2 Bring a large pan of salted water to the boil. Add the potatoes and pasta. Stir well and let the water return to the boil. Lower the heat and simmer for 15 minutes, or according to the instructions on the packet, until the pasta is cooked.

3 Heat the remaining oil in a large pan, add the rest of the onion and the garlic and fry for 2–3 minutes, stirring occasionally. Add the rocket, toss over the heat for about 2 minutes, or until wilted, then stir in the tomato sauce and the ricotta. Mix well.

4 Drain the pasta and potatoes, add them both to the pan of sauce and toss to mix. Taste the sauce for seasoning and then serve immediately in warmed bowls, with grated Pecorino offered separately.

CORIANDER OMELETTE PARCELS <u>WITH</u> ORIENTAL VEGETABLES

PIQUANT, STIR-FRIED VEGETABLES WITH GINGER, CHILLIES AND BLACK BEAN SAUCE ARE WRAPPED IN A LIGHT CORIANDER OMELETTE. THEY MAKE AN ATTRACTIVE AND FLAVOURSOME LUNCH.

SERVES FOUR

INGREDIENTS
   130g/4½oz broccoli, cut into
     small florets
   30ml/2 tbsp groundnut (peanut) oil
   1cm/½in piece fresh root ginger,
     finely grated
   1 large garlic clove, crushed
   2 fresh red chillies, seeded and
     finely sliced
   4 spring onions (scallions), sliced
     diagonally
   175g/6oz/3 cups shredded pak choi
     (bok choy)
   50g/2oz/2 cups fresh coriander
     (cilantro) leaves, plus extra
     to garnish
   115g/4oz/½ cup beansprouts
   45ml/3 tbsp black bean sauce
   4 eggs
   salt and ground black pepper

1 Blanch the broccoli in boiling salted water for 2 minutes, drain, then refresh under cold running water.

2 Meanwhile, heat 15ml/1 tbsp of the oil in a frying pan or wok. Add the ginger, garlic and half the chilli and stir-fry for 1 minute. Add the spring onions (scallions), broccoli and pak choi (bok choy), and stir-fry for 2 minutes more, tossing the vegetables continuously to prevent sticking and to cook them evenly.

3 Chop three-quarters of the coriander (cilantro) and add to the frying pan or wok. Add the beansprouts, stir-fry for 1 minute, then add the black bean sauce and heat through for 1 minute more. Remove the pan from the heat and keep warm.

4 Mix the eggs lightly with a fork and season them well. Heat a little of the remaining oil in a small frying pan and add a quarter of the beaten egg. Swirl the egg until it covers the base of the pan, then scatter over a quarter of the reserved coriander leaves. Cook until set, then turn out the omelette on to a plate and keep warm while you make three more omelettes, adding more oil, when necessary.

5 Spoon the vegetable stir-fry on to the omelettes and roll up. Cut in half crossways and serve garnished with coriander leaves and the remaining sliced chilli.

PARSNIPS AND CHICKPEAS IN GARLIC, ONION, CHILLI AND GINGER SAUCE

A SELECTION OF AROMATIC HERBS BLENDS WITH GROUND CASHEW NUTS TO MAKE A RICH AND SATISFYING, INDIAN-STYLE STEW. DELICIOUS ACCOMPANIED BY YOGURT AND BREAD.

SERVES FOUR

INGREDIENTS

200g/7oz/generous 1 cup dried
  chickpeas, soaked overnight in cold
  water, then drained
7 garlic cloves, finely chopped
1 small onion, chopped
5cm/2in piece of fresh root ginger,
  peeled and chopped
2 fresh green chillies, seeded and
  finely chopped
450ml/¾ pint/scant 2 cups plus
  75ml/5 tbsp water
60ml/4 tbsp groundnut (peanut) oil
5ml/1 tsp cumin seeds
10ml/2 tsp ground coriander seeds
5ml/1 tsp ground turmeric
2.5–5ml/½–1 tsp chilli powder or
  mild paprika
50g/2oz/⅓ cup cashew nuts, toasted
  and ground
250g/9oz tomatoes, peeled
  and chopped
900g/2lb parsnips, cut into chunks
5ml/1 tsp ground roasted
  cumin seeds
juice of 1 lime
salt and ground black pepper
To garnish
  fresh coriander (cilantro) leaves
  a few cashew nuts, toasted

1 Put the chickpeas in a pan, cover with cold water and bring to the boil. Boil vigorously for 10 minutes, then reduce the heat so that the water boils steadily, and cook for 1–1½ hours, or until tender. Drain. (Do not add salt as this will toughen the chickpeas.)

2 Set 10ml/2 tsp of the garlic aside, then place the remainder in a food processor or blender with the onion, ginger and half the chillies. Add 75ml/5 tbsp water and process to a paste.

3 Heat the oil in a frying pan and cook the cumin seeds for 30 seconds. Stir in the spices and ground cashew nuts.

4 Add the paste and cook, stirring, until the water begins to evaporate. Add the tomatoes and stir-fry until the mixture begins to turn red-brown.

5 Mix in the chickpeas and parsnips with the main batch of water, 5ml/1 tsp salt and plenty of black pepper. Bring to the boil, stir, then simmer, uncovered, for 15–20 minutes, or until the parsnips are tender.

6 Reduce, if necessary, by boiling fiercely until thick. Add the ground roasted cumin with more salt and lime juice to taste. Stir in the reserved garlic and chilli. Cook for 1–2 minutes. Sprinkle the coriander and toasted cashew nuts over, and serve. A yogurt dip makes a good accompaniment.

GARLIC AND HERB BREAD

THIS IRRESISTIBLE GARLIC BREAD INCLUDES PLENTY OF FRESH MIXED HERBS. YOU CAN VARY THE OVERALL FLAVOUR ACCORDING TO THE COMBINATION OF HERBS YOU CHOOSE.

SERVES THREE TO FOUR

INGREDIENTS
  1 baguette or bloomer loaf
For the garlic and herb butter
  115g/4oz/½ cup unsalted (sweet)
    butter, softened
  5–6 large garlic cloves, finely
    chopped or crushed
  30–45ml/2–3 tbsp chopped fresh
    herbs (such as parsley, chervil and
    a little tarragon)
  15ml/1 tbsp chopped fresh chives
  coarse salt and ground black pepper

1 Preheat the oven to 200°C/400°F/ Gas 6. Make the garlic and herb butter by beating the butter with the garlic, herbs, chives and seasoning.

VARIATIONS
• Use 105ml/7 tbsp extra virgin olive oil instead of the butter.
• Flavour the butter with garlic, a little chopped fresh chilli, grated (shredded) lime rind and chopped fresh coriander (cilantro).
• Add chopped, pitted black olives or sun-dried tomatoes to the butter with a little grated lemon rind.

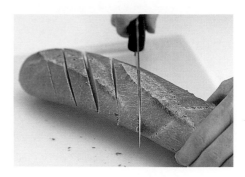

2 Cut the bread into 1cm/½in thick diagonal slices, but be sure to leave them attached at the base so that the loaf stays intact.

3 Spread the garlic and herb butter between the slices evenly, being careful not to detach them, and then spread any remaining butter over the top of the loaf.

4 Wrap the loaf in foil and bake in the preheated oven for 20–25 minutes, until the butter is melted and the crust is golden and crisp. Cut the loaf into slices to serve.

COOK'S TIP
This loaf makes an excellent addition to a barbecue. If space permits, place the foil-wrapped loaf on the top of the barbecue and cook for about the same length of time as for oven baking. Turn the foil parcel over several times to ensure it cooks evenly.

RED ONION, GORGONZOLA AND SAGE PIZZAS

THE TOPPING ON THESE INDIVIDUAL PIZZAS COMBINES THE RICHNESS OF GORGONZOLA WITH THE EARTHY FLAVOURS OF SAGE AND SWEET RED ONIONS.

SERVES FOUR

INGREDIENTS
  30ml/2 tbsp garlic oil
  2 small red onions
  150g/5oz Gorgonzola piccante cheese
  2 garlic cloves
  10ml/2 tsp chopped fresh sage
  ground black pepper
For the pizza dough
  175g/6oz/1½ cups strong white bread
    flour, plus extra for dusting
  1.5ml/¼ tsp salt
  5ml/1 tsp easy-blend (rapid-rise)
    dried yeast
  120–150ml/4–5fl oz/½–⅔ cup
    lukewarm water
  15ml/1 tbsp olive oil

1 To make the dough, sift the flour and salt into a bowl. Stir in the yeast. Make a well in the centre of the ingredients. Pour in the water and oil and mix to a soft dough.

2 Knead the dough on a lightly floured surface for about 10 minutes until smooth and elastic, then place in a greased bowl and cover with clear film. Leave in a warm place to rise for about 1 hour, or until doubled in size.

3 Knock back (punch down) the dough, and knead again for 2–3 minutes. Preheat the oven to 220°C/425°F/Gas 7. Divide the dough into eight and roll out each one on a lightly floured surface to a small oval about 5mm/¼in thick. Place well apart on two greased baking sheets and prick with a fork. Brush the bases with 15ml/1 tbsp of the oil.

4 Slice the onions into thin wedges. Scatter the slices over the pizza bases. Remove the rind from the Gorgonzola. Cut the cheese into small cubes, then scatter it over the onions.

5 Cut the garlic lengthways into thin strips and sprinkle over, along with the sage. Drizzle the remaining oil on top and grind over plenty of black pepper. Bake for 10–15 minutes, or until crisp and golden. Serve immediately.

Sweet Pear and Cardamom Sponge

Scented cardamom seeds complement dessert pears in this moist sponge. It makes a delicious dessert served with a dollop of whipped cream or ice cream.

SERVES FOUR

INGREDIENTS

115g/4oz/½ cup butter, softened,
  plus extra for greasing
115g/4oz/1 cup self-raising (self-
  rising) flour, plus extra for dusting
5 pears
10 green cardamom pods
5ml/1 tsp baking powder
115g/4oz/generous ½ cup caster
  (superfine) sugar
3 egg yolks
30–45ml/2–3 tbsp warm water

1 Preheat the oven to 190°C/375°F/Gas 5. Line the base of a 20cm/8in-diameter cake tin (pan) with greaseproof (waxed) paper and then butter and lightly flour the sides.

2 Peel the pears, cut them in half and remove the cores. Lay the fruit cut-side up in a circle in the bottom of the tin.

COOK'S TIP
Choose very sweet dessert pears, like Comice or Williams. They need to be completely ripe and very juicy.

3 Remove the cardamom seeds from the pods and crush the seeds lightly using a mortar and pestle.

4 Sift together the flour and baking powder. Add the sugar, the crushed cardamom seeds, butter, egg yolks and 30ml/2 tbsp of the water. Beat with an electric or hand whisk until creamy. The mixture should fall off a spoon; if it does not, add a little more water.

5 Place the mixture on top of the pears and level with a knife. Bake the cake for 45–60 minutes, or until firm.

6 Turn the cake out on to a wire rack and peel off the greaseproof paper. Cool before serving.

DATE AND WALNUT SPICE CAKE

NUTMEG, MIXED SPICE AND WALNUTS FLAVOUR THIS SCRUMPTIOUS CAKE, AND DATES MAKE IT DELICIOUSLY MOIST. IT GOES VERY WELL WITH MORNING COFFEE.

SERVES EIGHT

INGREDIENTS

   115g/4oz/½ cup unsalted (sweet) butter, plus extra for greasing
   175g/6oz/1½ cups unbleached self-raising (self-rising) flour, plus extra for dusting
   175g/6oz/¾ cup soft dark brown sugar
   2 eggs
   5ml/1 tsp bicarbonate of soda (baking soda)
   2.5ml/½ tsp freshly grated (shredded) nutmeg
   5ml/1 tsp mixed spice
   pinch of salt
   175ml/6fl oz/¾ cup buttermilk
   50g/2oz/⅓ cup ready-to-eat pitted dates, chopped
   25g/1oz/¼ cup chopped walnuts
For the topping
   60ml/4 tbsp clear honey
   45ml/3 tbsp fresh orange juice
   15ml/1 tbsp coarsely grated (shredded) orange rind, plus extra to decorate

1 Grease and lightly flour a 23cm/9in springform cake tin (pan). Preheat the oven to 180°C/350°F/Gas 4.

2 Cream together the butter and sugar until the mixture is fluffy and creamy. Add the eggs, one at a time, and then beat well to combine.

3 Sift together the flour, bicarbonate of soda, nutmeg, mixed spice and salt. Gradually add this to the creamed mixture, alternating with the buttermilk. Add the chopped dates and walnuts, and stir well.

4 Spoon the mixture into the prepared cake tin and level the top. Bake for 50 minutes, or until a skewer inserted into the centre comes out clean. Leave to cool for 5 minutes, then turn out on to a wire rack to cool completely.

5 To make the topping, heat the clear honey, orange juice and rind in a small, heavy pan. Bring to the boil and boil rapidly for 3 minutes, without stirring, until syrupy.

6 Make small holes over the top of the warm cake using the skewer, and then pour over the hot syrup. Decorate with the orange rind.

COOK'S TIP

To make a quite acceptable buttermilk substitute, simply mix 15ml/1 tbsp lemon juice with 250ml/8fl oz/1 cup semi-skimmed (low-fat) milk.

CINNAMON <u>AND</u> COFFEE PARFAIT

THIS FRENCH-STYLE ICE CREAM IS FLECKED WITH CINNAMON AND MIXED WITH JUST A HINT OF COFFEE. AS IT IS MADE WITH A BOILING SUGAR SYRUP IT DOESN'T REQUIRE BEATING DURING FREEZING, SO CAN BE POURED STRAIGHT INTO FREEZERPROOF SERVING DISHES.

SERVES SIX

INGREDIENTS

   15ml/1 tbsp instant coffee granules
   30ml/2 tbsp boiling water
   7.5ml/1½ tsp ground cinnamon
   4 egg yolks
   115g/4oz/generous ½ cup granulated
     sugar
   120ml/4fl oz/½ cup cold water
   300ml/½ pint/1¼ cups double
    (heavy) cream, lightly whipped
   200g/7oz/scant 1 cup crème fraîche
   extra ground cinnamon, to decorate

1 Spoon the coffee into a heatproof bowl, stir in the boiling water until dissolved, then stir in the cinnamon. Put the egg yolks in a large, heatproof bowl and whisk them lightly until frothy. Bring a medium pan of water to the boil and lower the heat so that it simmers gently.

2 Put the sugar in a small pan, add the cold water and heat gently, stirring occasionally, until the sugar has completely dissolved.

3 Increase the heat and boil for 4–5 minutes without stirring until the syrup registers 115ºC/239ºF on a sugar thermometer. Alternatively, test by dropping a little of the syrup into a cup of cold water. Pour the water away. If the syrup can be moulded to a soft ball, it is ready.

4 Put the bowl of egg yolks over the pan of simmering water and whisk in the sugar syrup. Whisk until the mixture is very thick and then remove from the heat. Continue whisking until it is cool.

5 Whisk the coffee and cinnamon into the yolk mixture, then fold in the cream and crème fraîche. Pour into a tub or individual freezerproof glass dishes. Freeze for 4 hours, or until firm. If frozen in a tub, scoop into bowls and decorate with a dusting of cinnamon.

COOK'S TIP
Test the syrup regularly. When it is nearly ready the syrup will fall slowly from the spoon. If the syrup fails to form a ball when tested in cold water, boil it for a few minutes more; if the syrup forms strands that snap it is overdone and you must start again.

GINGERED SEMI-FREDDO

THIS ICE CREAM IS LUXURIOUSLY CREAMY AND GENEROUSLY SPECKLED WITH CHOPPED STEM GINGER.
SEMI-FREDDO IS AN ITALIAN SEMI-FROZEN ICE CREAM THAT IS NEVER BEATEN DURING FREEZING. IT
WILL STAY SOFT WHEN FROZEN.

SERVES SIX

INGREDIENTS
  4 egg yolks
  115g/4oz/generous ½ cup caster
    (superfine) sugar
  120ml/4fl oz/½ cup cold water
  300ml/½ pint/1¼ cups double
    (heavy) cream
  115g/4oz/⅔ cup drained stem
    (crystallized) ginger, finely chopped,
    plus extra slices, to decorate
  45ml/3 tbsp whisky (optional)

1 Put the egg yolks in a large, heatproof bowl and whisk until frothy. Bring a pan of water to the boil and simmer gently.

2 Mix the sugar and measured cold water in a pan and heat gently, stirring occasionally, until the sugar has completely dissolved.

3 Increase the heat and boil for 4–5 minutes without stirring until the syrup registers 115°C/239°F on a sugar thermometer. Alternatively, test by dropping a little of the syrup into a cup of cold water. Pour the water away. You should be able to mould the syrup into a ball.

4 Put the bowl of egg yolks over the pan of simmering water and whisk in the sugar syrup. Continue whisking until the mixture is very thick. Remove from the heat and whisk until cool.

5 Whip the cream and lightly fold it into the yolk mixture, with the chopped ginger and whisky, if using. Pour into a plastic tub or similar freezerproof container and freeze for 1 hour.

6 Stir the semi-freddo to bring any ginger that has sunk to the bottom of the tub to the top, then return to the freezer for 5–6 hours, or until firm. Scoop into dishes or chocolate cases (see Cook's Tip). Decorate with slices of ginger.

COOK'S TIP
Semi-freddo looks wonderful in chocolate cases, made by spreading melted chocolate over squares of non-stick baking paper and then draping them over upturned tumblers. Peel the paper off when the chocolate has set and turn the cases the right way up before filling.

WINTER

Not only do the cold winds of winter make us all feel hungrier, but we also crave more robust flavours in our food. Fresh herbs continue to have a central role in the kitchen, but this is the season to combine them with other strong-tasting ingredients, such as spices, condiments, citrus juice and even liqueurs. What could be more welcoming for dinner party guests than Medallions of Venison with Herby Horseradish Dumplings, more satisfying for a family lunch than Liver Pâté Pie with Mustard and Parsley, or tastier than Herby Thai Tempeh Cakes with Sweet Dipping Sauce?

A versatile herb, parsley might be considered more useful in the winter than at any other time of year, providing a fresh green taste and a decorative garnish to all kinds of  dishes. Strongly flavoured herbs, such as thyme, rosemary and garlic, are also good choices for enhancing winter dishes, while mint, although often associated with summer cooking, is superb. Its slightly spicy flavour traditionally complements lamb, but it goes well with a wide range of other ingredients from aubergines (eggplant) to fish. If you haven't tried it, Syrian Onion Bread with Mint and Spices will be a revelation.

Baking, especially home-made bread, is a popular activity in the winter kitchen. There is something wonderfully comforting about the process, and the aroma as a loaf bakes is indescribably delicious. Who could resist Red Onion and Rosemary Focaccia served still warm from the oven?

Dried herbs are a useful stand-by in the winter and certainly better than no herbs at all. However, most supermarkets stock a year-round supply of fresh herbs that can keep the cook supplied when home-grown herbs are dormant or will need  replanting in the spring. Their intensity of aroma and flavour will never quite match that of freshly picked herbs, but they will provide that extra lift that is so important in winter.

LEEK, POTATO AND ROCKET SOUP

ROCKET ADDS ITS DISTINCTIVE, PEPPERY TASTE TO THIS WONDERFULLY SATISFYING SOUP. SERVE IT HOT, GARNISHED WITH A GENEROUS SPRINKLING OF TASTY CIABATTA CROÛTONS.

SERVES FOUR TO SIX

INGREDIENTS
   50g/2oz/¼ cup butter
   1 onion, chopped
   3 leeks, chopped
   2 medium floury potatoes, diced
   900ml/1½ pints/3¾ cups light
      chicken stock or water
   2 large handfuls of rocket (arugula),
      roughly chopped
   150ml/¼ pint/⅔ cup double (heavy)
      cream
   salt and ground black pepper
   garlic-flavoured ciabatta croûtons,
      to serve (see Cook's Tip)

1 Melt the butter in a large, heavy pan then add the chopped onion and leeks and the diced potatoes. Stir until the vegetables are coated in melted butter. Heat the ingredients until they are sizzling then reduce the heat to low.

2 Cover and sweat the vegetables for 15 minutes. Pour in the chicken stock or water and bring to the boil then reduce the heat, cover again and allow to simmer for 20 minutes, or until the vegetables are tender.

3 Press the soup through a sieve or pass through a food mill and return to the rinsed-out pan. (When puréeing the soup, don't use a food processor or blender, as these will give the soup a gluey texture.) Add the chopped rocket to the pan.

4 Allow the soup to cook gently, uncovered, for 5 minutes.

5 Stir in the cream, then season to taste and reheat gently. Ladle into warmed bowls and serve with a scattering of garlic-flavoured ciabatta croûtons.

COOK'S TIP
For the croûtons, cut 1cm/½in cubes of ciabatta bread. Heat a peeled garlic clove in 60ml/4 tbsp olive oil. Remove, then fry the croûtons until golden.

POTATO AND GARLIC BROTH

ALTHOUGH THERE IS PLENTY OF GARLIC IN THIS SOUP, THE END RESULT IS NOT OVERPOWERING.
SERVE PIPING HOT WITH BREAD, AS THE PERFECT WINTER WARMER.

SERVES FOUR

INGREDIENTS
  2 small or 1 large whole head of
    garlic (about 20 cloves)
  4 potatoes, diced
  1.75 litres/3 pints/7½ cups
    vegetable stock
  salt and ground black pepper
  chopped flat leaf parsley, to garnish
    (optional)

VARIATION
Make the soup more substantial by
placing in each bowl a slice of French
bread which has been toasted and
topped with melted cheese. Pour the
soup over so that the bread soaks it up.

1 Preheat the oven to 190°C/375°F/
Gas 5. Place the unpeeled garlic bulbs
or bulb in a small roasting pan and
bake for 30 minutes, or until they are
soft in the centre.

2 Meanwhile, par-boil the potatoes in a
large pan of boiling, lightly salted water
for 10 minutes.

3 Simmer the stock for 5 minutes. Drain
the par-boiled potatoes and then add to
the stock.

4 Squeeze the garlic pulp into the soup,
reserving a few cloves to garnish, stir
and season to taste. Simmer the soup
for 15 minutes and serve garnished with
garlic cloves and parsley, if you like.

LIVER PÂTÉ PIE <u>WITH</u> MUSTARD <u>AND</u> PARSLEY

A PORK AND HAM PÂTÉ IS FLAVOURED WITH ONION, MUSTARD, PARSLEY AND KIRSCH IN THIS RICH AND SATISFYING PIE. DELICIOUS SERVED FOR LUNCH WITH A GLASS OF PILSNER BEER.

3 Process half the minced (ground) pork and the liver until fairly smooth. Stir in the remaining pork, ham, onion, parsley, mustard, Kirsch and seasoning. Spoon the filling into the tin, smoothing it down and levelling the surface.

SERVES TEN

INGREDIENTS
  675g/1½lb minced (ground) pork
  350g/12oz pork liver
  350g/12oz/2 cups diced cooked ham
  1 small onion, finely chopped
  30ml/2 tbsp chopped fresh parsley
  5ml/1 tsp German mustard
  30ml/2 tbsp Kirsch
  salt and ground black pepper
  beaten egg, for sealing and glazing
  25g/1oz sachet aspic jelly
  250ml/8fl oz/1 cup boiling water
  mustard, bread and dill pickles,
    to serve
For the pastry
  450g/1lb/4 cups plain (all-purpose)
    flour, plus extra for dusting
  pinch of salt
  275g/10oz/1¼ cups butter
  2 eggs and 1 egg yolk
  30ml/2 tbsp water

1 Preheat the oven to 200°C/400°F/ Gas 6. To make the pastry, sift the flour and salt and rub in the butter. Beat the eggs, egg yolk and water, add to the dry ingredients and mix.

2 Knead the dough briefly until smooth. Roll out two-thirds on a lightly floured surface and use to line a 10 × 25cm/ 4 × 10in loaf tin (pan). Trim any excess dough neatly from around the edges.

4 Roll out the remaining pastry on the lightly floured surface and use it to top the pie, sealing the edges with some of the beaten egg. Decorate with the pastry trimmings and glaze with the remaining beaten egg. Using a fork, make three or four holes in the top, for the steam to escape.

5 Bake for 40 minutes, then reduce the oven temperature to 180°C/350°F/Gas 4 and cook for a further 1 hour. Cover the pastry with foil if the top begins to brown too much. Allow to cool in the tin.

6 Make up the aspic jelly, using the boiling water. Stir to dissolve. When it is cool, make a small hole near the edge of the pie with a skewer, then pour in the aspic through a greaseproof- (waxed-) paper funnel. Chill for at least 2 hours before serving the pie in slices with mustard, bread and dill pickles.

LENTIL AND SPINACH SALAD WITH ONION, CUMIN AND GARLIC

THIS EARTHY SALAD IS A BLEND OF HERBY FLAVOURS. PUY LENTILS ARE TOSSED WITH ONIONS, BAY, THYME, PARSLEY AND CUMIN AND THEN DRESSED IN A MEDLEY OF MUSTARD, GARLIC AND LEMON.

SERVES SIX

INGREDIENTS
225g/8oz/1 cup Puy lentils
1 fresh bay leaf
1 celery stick
fresh thyme sprig
30ml/2 tbsp olive oil
1 onion or 3–4 shallots, finely chopped
10ml/2 tsp crushed toasted
  cumin seeds
400g/14oz young spinach
30–45ml/2–3 tbsp chopped
  fresh parsley
toasted French bread, to serve
salt and ground black pepper
For the dressing
75ml/5 tbsp extra virgin olive oil
5ml/1 tsp Dijon mustard
15–25ml/1–1½ tbsp red wine vinegar
1 small garlic clove, finely chopped
2.5ml/½ tsp finely grated (shredded)
  lemon rind

1 Rinse the lentils and place them in a large pan. Add plenty of water to cover. Tie the bay leaf, celery and thyme into a bundle and add to the pan, then bring to the boil. Reduce the heat so that the water just boils steadily. Cook the lentils for 30–45 minutes, or until just tender. Do not add salt at this stage, as it toughens the lentils.

2 Meanwhile, to make the dressing, mix the oil, mustard and 15ml/1 tbsp vinegar with the garlic and lemon rind, and season well with salt and pepper.

3 Thoroughly drain the lentils and turn them into a bowl. Add most of the dressing and toss well, then set the lentils aside, stirring occasionally.

COOK'S TIP

Named after Puy in France, these small, greyish-green lentils are considered to have the best and most distinctive flavour. They keep both their shape and colour well when cooked.

4 Heat the olive oil in a pan or deep frying pan and sauté the chopped onion or shallots over a low heat for 4–5 minutes, or until they are beginning to soften. Add the cumin and cook for a further 1 minute.

5 Add the spinach and season to taste, then cover and cook for 2 minutes. Stir and cook again briefly until wilted.

6 Stir the spinach into the lentils and leave the salad to cool. Bring back to room temperature, if necessary. Stir in the remaining dressing and chopped parsley. Adjust the seasoning, and add extra red wine vinegar, if necessary.

7 Turn the salad on to a serving platter and serve with slices of toasted French bread.

BAKED COD WITH HORSERADISH SAUCE

FISH KEEPS MOIST WHEN BAKED IN A SAUCE. IN THIS UKRAINIAN RECIPE, A CREAMY HORSERADISH SAUCE IS SERVED ALONGSIDE, FOR ADDED FLAVOUR.

2 Melt the butter in a small, heavy pan. Stir in the flour and cook for 3–4 minutes, or until lightly golden. Stir to stop the flour sticking to the pan. Remove from the heat.

3 Gradually whisk the milk, and then the fish stock, into the flour mixture. Season with salt and ground black pepper. Bring to the boil, stirring, and simmer for 3 minutes, still stirring.

4 Pour the sauce over the fish and bake for 20–25 minutes, depending on the thickness. Check by gently inserting a knife into the thickest part: the flesh should be opaque.

5 For the horseradish sauce, blend the tomato purée and horseradish with the sour cream in a small pan. Slowly bring to the boil, stirring, and then simmer for 1 minute.

6 Pour the horseradish sauce into a serving bowl and serve alongside the baked fish. Serve the fish immediately. Garnish with the parsley sprigs and serve with potato wedges and fried sliced leeks.

SERVES FOUR

INGREDIENTS
    4 thick cod fillets or steaks
    15ml/1 tbsp lemon juice
    25g/1oz/2 tbsp butter
    25g/1oz/¼ cup plain (all-purpose)
      flour, sifted
    150ml/¼ pint/⅔ cup milk
    150ml/¼ pint/⅔ cup fish stock
    salt and ground black pepper
    sprigs of flat leaf parsley, to garnish
    potato wedges and fried sliced leeks,
      to serve
For the horseradish sauce
    30ml/2 tbsp tomato purée (paste)
    30ml/2 tbsp grated (shredded)
      fresh horseradish
    150ml/¼ pint/⅔ cup sour cream

1 Preheat the oven to 180°C/350°F/ Gas 4. Place the fish in a buttered ovenproof dish in a single layer. Sprinkle with lemon juice.

HERBY FISHCAKES WITH LEMON AND CHIVE SAUCE

THESE PIQUANT FISHCAKES ARE A CUT ABOVE THE REST. FLAVOURED WITH HORSERADISH AND PARSLEY, THEY ARE SERVED WITH A FRAGRANT GINGER, LEMON AND CHIVE SAUCE.

SERVES FOUR

INGREDIENTS
  350g/12oz potatoes, peeled
  75ml/5 tbsp milk
  350g/12oz haddock or hoki
    fillets, skinned
  15ml/1 tbsp lemon juice
  15ml/1 tbsp creamed horseradish
  30ml/2 tbsp chopped fresh parsley
  flour, for dusting
  115g/4oz/2 cups fresh wholemeal
    (whole-wheat) breadcrumbs
  salt and ground black pepper
  flat leaf parsley sprig, to garnish
  mangetouts (snow peas) and a sliced
    tomato and onion salad, to serve
For the lemon and chive sauce
  thinly pared rind and juice of
    ½ small lemon
  120ml/4fl oz/½ cup dry white wine
  2 thin slices fresh root ginger
  10ml/2 tsp cornflour (cornstarch)
  30ml/2 tbsp chopped fresh chives

1 Cook the potatoes in a large pan of boiling water for 15–20 minutes. Drain and mash with the milk, and season with salt and ground black pepper to taste.

2 Purée the fish together with the lemon juice and horseradish sauce in a food processor or blender. Mix together with the potatoes and parsley.

3 With floured hands, shape the mixture into eight fishcakes and coat with the breadcrumbs. Chill in the refrigerator for 30 minutes.

4 Cook the fishcakes under a preheated moderate grill (broiler) for 8 minutes on each side, or until browned.

5 To make the sauce, cut the lemon rind into strips and put into a pan with the lemon juice, wine and ginger and seasoning. Simmer for 6 minutes.

6 Blend the cornflour with 15ml/1 tbsp of cold water. Add to the pan and simmer until clear. Stir in the chives immediately before serving. Serve the sauce hot with the fishcakes, garnished with flat leaf parsley and accompanied by mangetouts and a tomato and onion salad.

SMOKED HADDOCK FILLETS <u>WITH</u> QUICK PARSLEY SAUCE

A GOOD, STRONG, FRESH PARSLEY SAUCE IS GREAT WITH FULL-FLAVOURED SMOKED HADDOCK. THIS RECIPE IS QUICK TO PREPARE AND MAKES A TASTY MIDWEEK MEAL.

<u>SERVES FOUR</u>

INGREDIENTS
    4 smoked haddock fillets, about
      225g/8oz each
    75g/3oz/6 tbsp butter, softened
    25g/1oz/¼ cup plain (all-purpose) flour
    300ml/½ pint/1¼ cups milk
    60ml/4 tbsp chopped fresh parsley
    salt and ground black pepper
    parsley sprigs, to garnish

1 Smear the fish on both sides with 50g/2oz/¼ cup butter. Preheat the grill (broiler).

2 Beat the remaining 25g/1oz butter and flour together with a wooden spoon to make a thick and smooth paste.

3 Grill (broil) the fish over a medium high heat for 10–15 minutes, turning when necessary.

4 Meanwhile, heat the milk until just below boiling point. Add the flour mixture in small knobs, whisking constantly over the heat. Continue until the sauce is smooth and thick.

5 Stir in the seasoning and parsley, and serve poured over the fillets, or in a serving jug. Serve immediately, garnished with parsley and your choice of vegetables.

ROAST VEAL <u>WITH</u> PARSLEY STUFFING

COOKING THIS JOINT OF VEAL, WITH ITS FRAGRANT PARSLEY AND LEEK STUFFING, IN A ROASTING BAG ENSURES THAT IT IS SUCCULENT AND FULL FLAVOURED WHEN SERVED.

SERVES SIX

INGREDIENTS
   25g/1oz/2 tbsp butter
   15ml/1 tbsp sunflower oil
   1 leek, finely chopped
   1 celery stick, finely chopped
   50g/2oz/1 cup fresh white
     breadcrumbs
   50g/2oz/½ cup chopped fresh flat
     leaf parsley
   900g/2lb boned loin of veal
   salt and ground black pepper
   gravy, sautéed potatoes, asparagus
     and mangetouts, to serve

1 Preheat the oven to 180°C/350°F/ Gas 4. Heat the butter and oil in a frying pan until foaming. Cook the leek and celery until they are just starting to colour, then remove the pan from the heat and stir in the breadcrumbs, parsley and seasoning.

2 Lay the joint of veal out flat. Spread the stuffing over the meat, then roll it up carefully and tie the joint at regular intervals to secure it in a neat shape.

VARIATION
Other mild herbs can be used in the stuffing instead of parsley. Try tarragon, chervil and chives, but avoid strong-flavoured herbs, such as marjoram, oregano and thyme, which tend to overpower the delicate flavour of veal.

3 Place the veal in a roasting bag and close the bag with an ovenproof tie, then place it in a roasting pan. Roast the veal for 1¼ hours.

4 Pierce the joint with a metal skewer to check whether it is cooked: when cooked the meat juices will run clear. Leave to stand for 10–15 minutes, then carve it into thick slices. Serve with a light gravy, sautéed potatoes, asparagus and mangetouts.

BEEF STROGANOFF WITH CHANTERELLE MUSHROOMS AND PARSLEY CREAM

DIJON MUSTARD AND PARSLEY ARE THE ESSENTIAL HERBS THAT FLAVOUR THE CREAMY SAUCE IN THIS FAMOUS DISH. CHANTERELLE MUSHROOMS AND FILLET BEEF MAKE IT AN EXQUISITE CHOICE FOR A DINNER-PARTY, ALTHOUGH BUTTON OR CUP MUSHROOMS COULD BE SUBSTITUTED IF NECESSARY.

SERVES FOUR

INGREDIENTS
450g/1lb fillet or rump steak,
    trimmed and cut into thin strips
30ml/2 tbsp olive oil
45ml/3 tbsp brandy
2 shallots, finely chopped
225g/8oz/3¼ cups chanterelle
    mushrooms, trimmed and halved
150ml/¼ pint/⅔ cup beef stock
75ml/5 tbsp sour cream
5ml/1 tsp Dijon mustard
½ sweet gherkin, chopped
45ml/3 tbsp chopped fresh parsley
salt and ground black pepper
buttered noodles dressed with poppy
    seeds, to serve

1 Season the steak with pepper, heat half of the oil in a pan and cook for 2 minutes. Transfer to a plate.

COOK'S TIP
Fillet steak will give the best flavour and texture, but rump or sirloin would also work well.

2 Place the pan over a high heat to brown the sediment. Add the brandy, and carefully ignite with a match to burn off the alcohol. Pour these juices over the meat, cover and keep warm.

3 Wipe the pan, heat the remaining oil and lightly brown the shallots. Add the mushrooms and sauté for 3–4 minutes.

4 Add the stock, simmer for a few minutes, then add the cream, mustard and gherkin together with the steak and its juices. Simmer briefly, season, and stir in the parsley. Serve with buttered noodles dressed with poppy seeds.

PAN-FRIED PORK <u>WITH</u> THYME <u>AND</u> GARLIC RISOTTO

LEAN PORK CHUMP CHOPS ARE DELICIOUS MARINATED IN GARLIC AND LEMON. SERVED WITH A SMOOTH, CREAMY, BUT ROBUST, RISOTTO, VIBRANTLY FLAVOURED WITH GARLIC AND THYME, THEY MAKE A TASTY MEAL.

3 To make the risotto, heat the butter with the oil in a large, heavy pan until foaming. Sauté the chopped shallots and garlic gently until the shallots are softened, but not coloured. Add the rice and thyme and stir until the grains are well coated.

4 Add a ladleful of boiling stock and cook gently, stirring occasionally. When all the stock is absorbed, add another ladleful. Continue cooking in this way until all the stock is absorbed. Keep the stock simmering and do not add too much at a time. This should take 25–30 minutes. Season to taste.

<u>SERVES FOUR</u>

INGREDIENTS
   4 large pork chump or loin chops, each weighing about 175g/6oz, rind removed
   1 garlic clove, finely chopped
   juice of ½ lemon
   5ml/1 tsp soft light brown sugar
   25g/1oz/2 tbsp butter
   fresh thyme sprigs, to garnish
For the risotto
   25g/1oz/2 tbsp butter
   15ml/1 tbsp olive oil
   2 shallots, chopped
   2 garlic cloves, finely chopped
   250g/9oz/1⅓ cups risotto rice
   15ml/1 tbsp fresh thyme leaves
   900ml/1½ pints/3¾ cups boiling pork or chicken stock
   salt and ground black pepper

1 Put the chops in a shallow dish and sprinkle the garlic over. To make the marinade, mix the lemon juice and soft light brown sugar together, and drizzle this over the chops.

2 Turn the chops to coat both sides with the lemon mixture, then cover the dish and leave them to marinate in the refrigerator while making the risotto.

5 Cook the chops when the risotto is half cooked. Melt the butter in a large, heavy frying pan. Remove the chops from the marinade, allowing the lemon juice to drip off, and fry them for 3–4 minutes on each side.

6 Divide the risotto among four plates and arrange the chops on top. Serve at once, garnished with fresh thyme.

MEDALLIONS OF VENISON WITH HERBY HORSERADISH DUMPLINGS

VENISON IS LEAN AND FULL-FLAVOURED AND IS ESPECIALLY DELICIOUS SERVED WITH THESE HORSERADISH AND HERB DUMPLINGS. THIS RECIPE MAKES A SPECTACULAR MAIN COURSE TO SERVE AT A DINNER PARTY AND IS ACTUALLY VERY EASY TO PREPARE.

SERVES FOUR

INGREDIENTS
  600ml/1 pint/2½ cups venison stock
  120ml/4fl oz/½ cup port
  15ml/1 tbsp sunflower oil
  4 medallions of venison, about
    175g/6oz each
  chopped parsley, to garnish
  steamed baby vegetables, such as
    carrots, courgettes (zucchini) and
    turnips, cooked, to serve
For the dumplings
  75g/3oz/⅔ cup self-raising (self-
    rising) flour
  40g/1½oz beef suet
  15ml/1 tbsp chopped fresh mixed herbs
  5ml/1 tsp creamed horseradish
  45–60ml/3–4 tbsp water
  salt and ground black pepper

1 To make the dumplings, mix together the flour, beef suet, mixed herbs and seasoning, and make a well in the middle. Add the creamed horseradish and water, then mix to make a soft but not sticky dough. Shape the dough into walnut-size balls and chill in the refrigerator for up to 1 hour.

2 Boil the venison stock in a pan until reduced by half. Add the port and continue boiling until reduced again by half, then pour the reduced stock into a large frying pan. Heat the stock until it is simmering and add the dumplings. Poach them gently for 5–10 minutes, or until risen and cooked through. Use a draining spoon to remove the dumplings from the pan.

3 Smear the oil over a non-stick griddle and heat until very hot. Add the venison medallions and cook them for 2–3 minutes on each side. Remove from the pan. Place them on warm serving plates and pour the sauce over. Serve with the dumplings and the baby vegetables, garnished with chopped parsley.

HERBY THAI TEMPEH CAKES WITH SWEET DIPPING SAUCE

MADE FROM SOYA BEANS, TEMPEH IS SIMILAR TO TOFU BUT HAS A NUTTIER TASTE. HERE, IT IS COMBINED WITH A FRAGRANT BLEND OF LEMON GRASS, CHILLIES AND GINGER AND FORMED INTO SMALL PATTIES.

<u>MAKES EIGHT CAKES</u>

INGREDIENTS
1 lemon grass stalk, outer leaves removed and inside finely chopped
2 garlic cloves, chopped
2 spring onions (scallions), finely chopped
2 shallots, roughly chopped
2 fresh chillies, seeded and finely chopped
2.5cm/1in piece fresh root ginger, finely chopped
60ml/4 tbsp chopped fresh coriander, (cilantro) plus extra to garnish
250g/9oz tempeh, thawed if frozen, sliced
15ml/1 tbsp lime juice
5ml/1 tsp caster (superfine) sugar
45ml/3 tbsp plain (all-purpose) flour
1 large egg, lightly beaten
vegetable oil, for frying
salt and ground black pepper
For the dipping sauce
45ml/3 tbsp mirin
45ml/3 tbsp white wine vinegar
2 spring onions (scallions), finely sliced
15ml/1 tbsp sugar
2 fresh chillies, finely chopped
30ml/2 tbsp chopped fresh coriander
large pinch of salt

1 To make the sauce, mix all the ingredients in a bowl and set aside.

2 Place the lemon grass, garlic, spring onions, shallots, chillies, ginger and coriander in a food processor or blender; process the mixture to form a coarse paste.

3 Add the tempeh, lime juice and sugar to the processor or blender, then process until the ingredients are well combined. Add the seasoning, flour and beaten egg. Process again until the mixture forms a coarse, sticky paste.

4 Using one heaped serving-spoonful of the tempeh mixture at a time, form into rounds with your hands – the mixture will be quite sticky.

5 Heat enough oil to cover the base of a large frying pan. Fry the tempeh cakes in batches for 5–6 minutes, turning once, until they are golden. Drain on kitchen paper and serve warm with the dipping sauce, garnished with the reserved coriander.

COOK'S TIP
Mirin is a sweet, almost syrupy Japanese rice wine brewed specially for cooking purposes. Buy it from good Oriental grocers.

PENNE WITH AUBERGINE AND MINT PESTO

WALNUTS, MINT AND PARSLEY MAKE A SPLENDID AND UNUSUAL VARIATION ON THE CLASSIC ITALIAN PESTO. HERE IT IS TOSSED INTO PASTA AND AUBERGINES, WHERE THE MINTY AROMA IS EMPHASIZED.

SERVES FOUR

INGREDIENTS
  2 large aubergines (eggplant)
  450g/1lb penne
  50g/2oz/⅓ cup walnut halves
  salt
For the pesto
  25g/1oz/1 cup fresh mint leaves
  15g/½oz/½ cup flat leaf parsley
  40g/1½oz/scant ⅓ cup walnuts
  40g/1½oz/½ cup freshly grated
    (shredded) Parmesan cheese
  2 garlic cloves
  90ml/6 tbsp olive oil
  salt and ground black pepper

1 Cut the aubergines lengthways into 1cm/½in slices, then cut the slices crossways into short strips.

2 Layer the strips in a colander with salt and leave to stand for 30 minutes over a plate to catch any juices. Rinse well in cool water and drain.

3 Place all the pesto ingredients, except the oil, in a blender or food processor.

4 Blend until smooth, then gradually add the oil in a thin stream until the mixture amalgamates. Season to taste with salt and ground black pepper.

5 Cook the pasta in boiling salted water according to the packet instructions. Add the aubergine 3 minutes before the end.

6 Drain well and mix in the mint pesto and walnut halves. Serve immediately.

GRILLED POLENTA WITH CARAMELIZED ONIONS, RADICCHIO AND THYME

SLICES OF GRILLED POLENTA ARE TASTY TOPPED WITH SLOWLY CARAMELIZED ONIONS FLAVOURED WITH GARLIC, THYME AND BUBBLING TALEGGIO CHEESE, IN THIS DISH FROM NORTHERN ITALY.

SERVES FOUR

INGREDIENTS
900ml/1½ pints/3¾ cups water
150g/5oz/1¼ cups polenta
  or corn meal
50g/2oz/⅔ cup freshly grated
  (shredded) Parmesan cheese
5ml/1 tsp chopped fresh thyme
90ml/6 tbsp olive oil
675g/1½lb onions, halved and sliced
2 garlic cloves, chopped
a few fresh thyme sprigs
5ml/1 tsp brown sugar
30ml/2 tbsp balsamic vinegar
2 heads radicchio, cut into thick
  slices or wedges
225g/8oz Taleggio cheese, sliced
salt and ground black pepper

1 In a large pan, bring the water to the boil and add 5ml/1 tsp salt. Adjust the heat so that it simmers. Stirring all the time, add the polenta or corn meal in a steady stream, then bring to the boil. Cook over a very low heat, stirring frequently, for 30–40 minutes, or until thick and smooth.

2 Beat in the Parmesan and chopped thyme, then turn out the mixture on to a work surface or tray. Spread evenly, then leave to cool and set.

3 Heat 30ml/2 tbsp of the oil in a frying pan over a moderate heat. Add the onions and stir to coat in the oil, then cover and cook over a very low heat for 15 minutes, stirring occasionally.

4 Add the garlic and a few thyme sprigs and cook, uncovered, for 10 minutes, or until light brown and very soft. Add the sugar, 15ml/1 tbsp of the vinegar and salt and pepper. Cook for another 10 minutes, or until soft and well-browned. Taste and add more vinegar and seasoning as necessary.

5 Heat the grill (broiler). Cut the polenta into thick slices and brush with a little of the remaining oil, then grill (broil) until crusty and lightly browned.

6 Turn the polenta slices and add the wedges of radicchio to the grill rack (broiler) or pan. Season the radicchio and brush with a little oil. Grill until the polenta and radicchio are browned. Drizzle a little balsamic vinegar over the radicchio.

7 Heap the onions on to the polenta. Scatter the cheese and a few sprigs of thyme over both polenta and radicchio. Grill until the cheese is bubbling. Season to taste with ground black pepper and serve immediately.

RED ONION AND ROSEMARY FOCACCIA

THIS BREAD IS RICH IN OLIVE OIL AND IT HAS AN AROMATIC TOPPING OF RED ONION, FRESH ROSEMARY AND COARSE SALT.

2 Set the yeast aside in a warm, but not hot, place for 10 minutes, until it has turned frothy.

3 Add the yeast, the remaining water, 15ml/1 tbsp of the oil and the chopped rosemary to the flour. Mix all the ingredients together to form a dough, then gather the dough into a ball and knead on a floured work surface for about 5 minutes, until smooth and elastic. You may need to add a little extra flour if the dough is very sticky.

4 Place the dough in a lightly oiled bowl and slip it into a polythene bag or cover with oiled clear film and leave to rise. The length of time you leave it for depends on the temperature: leave it all day in a cool place, overnight in the refrigerator, or for 1–2 hours in a warm, but not hot, place.

5 Lightly oil a baking sheet. Knead the dough to form a flat loaf that is about 30cm/12in round or square. Place on the baking sheet, cover with oiled polythene or clear film and leave to rise again in a warm place for a further 40–60 minutes.

6 Preheat the oven to 220°C/425°F/ Gas 7. Toss the onion in 15ml/1 tbsp of the oil and scatter over the loaf with the rosemary sprigs and a scattering of coarse salt. Bake for 15–20 minutes until golden brown.

SERVES FOUR TO FIVE

INGREDIENTS
   450g/1lb/4 cups strong white bread
     flour, plus extra for dusting
   5ml/1 tsp salt
   7g/¼oz fresh yeast or generous 5ml/1
     tsp dried yeast
   2.5ml/½ tsp light muscovado
     (molasses) sugar
   250ml/8fl oz/1 cup lukewarm water
   60ml/4 tbsp extra virgin olive oil,
     plus extra for greasing
   5ml/1 tsp very finely chopped fresh
     rosemary, plus 6–8 small sprigs
   1 red onion, thinly sliced
   coarse salt

1 Sift the flour and salt into a bowl. Set aside. Cream the fresh yeast with the sugar, and gradually stir in half the water. If using dried yeast, stir the sugar into the water and sprinkle the dried yeast over.

SYRIAN ONION BREAD <u>WITH</u> MINT <u>AND</u> SPICES

FRESH MINT CONTRASTS WITH GROUND CUMIN AND CORIANDER SEEDS AND ONION TO TOP THESE SAVOURY BREADS FROM SYRIA. THEY MAKE AN EXCELLENT ACCOMPANIMENT FOR SOUPS OR SALADS.

MAKES EIGHT BREADS

INGREDIENTS
  450g/1lb/4 cups unbleached strong
    white bread flour, plus extra
    for dusting
  5ml/1 tsp salt
  20g/¾oz fresh yeast
  280ml/9fl oz/scant 1¼ cups
    lukewarm water
  oil, for greasing
For the topping
  60ml/4 tbsp finely chopped onion
  5ml/1 tsp ground cumin
  10ml/2 tsp ground coriander seeds
  10ml/2 tsp chopped fresh mint
  30ml/2 tbsp olive oil

4 Knock back (punch down) the dough and turn out on to a lightly floured surface. Divide into eight equal pieces and roll into 13–15cm/5–6in rounds. Make them slightly concave. Prick all over and space well apart on the baking sheets. Cover with lightly oiled clear film and leave to rise for 15–20 minutes.

5 Meanwhile, preheat the oven to 200°C/400°F/Gas 6. Mix the chopped onion, ground cumin, ground coriander and chopped mint in a bowl. Brush the breads with the olive oil for the topping, sprinkle evenly with the spicy onion mixture and bake for 15–20 minutes. Serve the onion breads warm.

1 Lightly flour two baking sheets. Sift the flour and salt together into a large bowl and make a well in the centre. Cream the yeast with a little of the water, then mix in the remainder.

2 Add the yeast mixture to the centre of the flour and mix to a firm dough. Turn out on to a lightly floured surface and knead for 8–10 minutes, or until smooth and elastic.

3 Place in a lightly oiled bowl, cover with lightly oiled clear film and leave to rise, in a warm place, for about 1 hour, or until doubled in size.

COOK'S TIP
If you haven't any fresh mint to hand, then add 15ml/1 tbsp dried mint. Use the freeze-dried variety if you can as it has much more flavour.

SOUR RYE BREAD WITH CARAWAY SEEDS

AROMATIC CARAWAY SEEDS TOP THIS EAST EUROPEAN BREAD. IT USES A SOURDOUGH "STARTER", WHICH NEEDS TO BE MADE A DAY OR TWO IN ADVANCE.

MAKES TWO LOAVES

INGREDIENTS
    450g/1lb/4 cups rye flour
    450g/1lb/4 cups strong white bread
      flour, plus extra for dusting
    15ml/1 tbsp salt
    7g/¼oz sachet easy-blend (rapid-rise)
      dried yeast
    25g/1oz/2 tbsp butter, softened, plus
      extra for greasing
    600ml/1 pint/2½ cups warm water
    15ml/1 tbsp caraway seeds
For the sourdough starter
    60ml/4 tbsp rye flour
    45ml/3 tbsp warm milk

1 For the starter, mix the rye flour and milk in a bowl. Cover with clear film. Leave in a warm place for 1–2 days.

2 Sift together both types of flour and the salt into a large mixing bowl. Stir in the easy-blend dried yeast. Make a well in the centre of the dry ingredients and add the butter, warm water and sourdough starter. Mix well with a wooden spoon until you have formed a soft dough.

3 Turn out the dough on to a lightly floured surface and knead for about 10 minutes, or until smooth and elastic. Put in a clean bowl, cover with greased clear film and leave to rise in a warm place for 1 hour, or until doubled in size.

4 Knead for 1 minute, then divide the dough in half. Shape each piece into a round 15cm/6in across. Transfer to two greased baking sheets. Cover with greased clear film and leave the loaves to rise for 30 minutes.

5 Preheat the oven to 200°C/400°F/ Gas 6. Brush the loaves with water, then sprinkle with caraway seeds.

6 Bake for 35–40 minutes, or until the loaves are browned and sound hollow when tapped on the bottom. Cool on a wire rack.

COOK'S TIP
Sour rye bread keeps fresh for up to a week. This recipe can also be made without yeast, but the resulting bread will be much denser.

POPPY-SEED ROLL

THIS SWEET YEAST BAKE WITH ITS SPIRAL FILLING OF DRIED FRUITS, POPPY SEEDS AND LEMON IS A WONDERFUL EXAMPLE OF TRADITIONAL POLISH COOKING. IT MAKES AN UNUSUAL PASTRY TO SERVE WITH AFTERNOON TEA.

SERVES TWELVE

INGREDIENTS
450g/1lb/4 cups plain (all-purpose)
   flour, plus extra for dusting
pinch of salt
30ml/2 tbsp caster (superfine) sugar
10ml/2 tsp easy-blend (rapid-rise)
   dried yeast
175ml/6fl oz/¾ cup milk
finely grated (shredded) rind of 1 lemon
50g/2oz/¼ cup butter
For the filling and glaze
50g/2oz/¼ cup butter
115g/4oz/⅔ cup poppy seeds
50ml/2fl oz/¼ cup set (crystallized)
   honey
65g/2½oz/½ cup raisins
65g/2½oz/scant ½ cup finely
   chopped candied orange peel
50g/2oz/½ cup ground almonds
1 egg yolk
50g/2oz/¼ cup caster (superfine) sugar
oil, for greasing
15ml/1 tbsp milk
60ml/4 tbsp apricot jam
15ml/1 tbsp lemon juice
15ml/1 tbsp rum or brandy
25g/1oz/¼ cup toasted flaked
   (sliced) almonds

1 Sift the flour, salt and sugar into a bowl. Stir in the easy-blend dried yeast. Make a well in the centre.

2 Heat the milk and lemon rind in a pan with the butter, until melted. Cool a little, then add to the dry ingredients and mix to a dough.

3 Knead the dough on a lightly floured surface for 10 minutes, until smooth and elastic. Put the dough in a clean bowl, cover and leave in a warm place to rise for 45–50 minutes, or until doubled in size.

4 For the filling, melt the butter in a pan. Reserve 15ml/1 tbsp of the poppy seeds, then process the rest in a food processor.

5 Add the processed poppy seeds to the pan with the honey, raisins and candied orange peel. Cook gently for 5 minutes. Stir in the ground almonds, then leave to cool.

6 Whisk the egg yolk and sugar together in a bowl until pale, then fold into the poppy seed mixture. Roll out the dough on a lightly floured surface to form a rectangle that measures 30 × 35cm/ 12 × 14in. Spread the filling to within 2.5cm/1in of the edges.

7 Roll both ends towards the centre. Place on a baking sheet, cover with oiled clear film and leave to rise for 30 minutes. Preheat the oven to 190°C/375°F/Gas 5.

8 Brush with the milk, then sprinkle with the reserved poppy seeds. Bake for 30 minutes, until golden brown.

9 Heat the jam and lemon juice gently until bubbling. Sieve, then stir in the rum or brandy. Brush over the roll while still warm and scatter with almonds.

DATE, FIG AND ORANGE PUDDING

THE FULL AND RICH FLAVOUR OF FIGS AND DATES IS HIGHLIGHTED BY ZESTY ORANGE IN THIS WARM AND COMFORTING PUDDING. IDEAL TO SERVE ON COLD, WINTRY DAYS.

2 Leave the fruit mixture to cool, then transfer to a food processor or blender and process until smooth. Press the mixture through a sieve to remove the fig seeds, if you wish.

3 Cream the butter and sugar until pale and fluffy, then beat in the fig purée. Beat in the eggs, then fold in the flours and mix until combined.

4 Grease a 1.5 litre/2½ pint/6¼ cup pudding basin, and pour in the golden syrup, if using. Tilt the bowl to cover the inside with a layer of syrup. Spoon in the pudding mixture. Cover the top with greaseproof (waxed) paper, with a pleat down the centre, and then with pleated foil, and tie down with string.

5 Place the bowl in a large pan and pour in enough water to come halfway up the sides of the bowl. Cover with a tight-fitting lid and steam for 2 hours. Check the water occasionally and top up if necessary.

6 Turn the pudding out and decorate with the reserved orange rind. Serve piping hot.

SERVES SIX

INGREDIENTS
 juice and grated (shredded) rind
  of 2 oranges
 115g/4oz/⅔ cup pitted, chopped,
  ready-to-eat dried dates
 115g/4oz/⅔ cup chopped ready-to-eat
  dried figs
 30ml/2 tbsp orange liqueur (optional)
 175g/6oz/¾ cup unsalted (sweet)
  butter, plus extra for greasing
 175g/6oz/¾ cup soft light brown sugar
 3 eggs
 75g/3oz/⅔ cup self-raising (self-rising)
  wholemeal (whole-wheat) flour
 115g/4oz/1 cup unbleached self-
  raising (self-rising) flour
 30ml/2 tbsp golden (light corn)
  syrup (optional)

1 Reserve a few strips of orange rind for the decoration and put the rest in a pan with the orange juice. Add the dates and figs, and orange liqueur, if using. Cook, covered, over a gentle heat for 8–10 minutes, or until soft.

SOUFFLÉED RICE PUDDING <u>WITH</u> NUTMEG

VANILLA AND NUTMEG ADD THEIR DELICATE FLAVOURS TO THIS CREAMY SOUFFLÉED RICE PUDDING. IT IS EQUALLY DELICIOUS SERVED COLD.

SERVES FOUR

INGREDIENTS

    65g/2½oz/⅓ cup short grain
      pudding rice
    45ml/3 tbsp clear honey
    750ml/1¼ pints/3 cups milk
    1 vanilla pod (bean) or 2.5ml/½ tsp
      vanilla essence (extract)
    butter, for greasing
    2 egg whites
    5ml/1 tsp freshly grated
      (shredded) nutmeg
    wafer biscuits (cookies),
      to serve (optional)

1 Place the rice, honey and milk in a heavy or non-stick pan, and bring the milk to just below boiling point, watching it closely to prevent it from boiling over. Add the vanilla pod, if using.

2 Reduce the heat to the lowest setting and cover the pan. Leave to cook for 1–1¼ hours, stirring occasionally to prevent sticking, until most of the liquid has been absorbed.

3 Remove the vanilla pod or, if using vanilla essence, add this to the rice mixture now. Preheat the oven to 220°C/425°F/Gas 7. Grease a 1 litre/ 1¾ pint/4 cup baking dish with butter.

COOK'S TIP

This pudding is especially delicious topped with a stewed, dried-fruit salad, although a fresh summer-fruit compote would also work well.

4 Place the egg whites in a large grease-free bowl and whisk them until they hold soft peaks. Using either a large metal spoon or a fish slice (spatula), fold the egg whites evenly into the rice and milk mixture. Tip into the baking dish.

5 Sprinkle with grated nutmeg and then bake in the oven for 15–20 minutes, or until the rice pudding has risen well and the surface is golden brown. Serve the rice pudding hot, with wafer biscuits, if you like.

INDEX